Someone To Watch Over Me

To Jackie

Someone To Watch Over Me

from

Jim Glazebrook DFC

Jim Glazebrook

with

Bob Swallow

With a foreword by Keith Jones
Chief Executive of Mission Aviation Fellowship UK

An Autobiography
incorporating a War History
of No. 206 Squadron Royal Air Force

and

a Summary of the origins and development
of Mission Aviation Fellowship worldwide

RoperPenberthy Publishing Ltd
Horsham, England

Published by RoperPenberthy Publishing Ltd
P O Box 545, Horsham, England

Sole distributor: Harvest Fields
Unit 17, Churchill Business Park, Churchill Road,
Doncaster, UK. DN1 2TF

ISBN 1 903905 23 0

Cover design by Angie Moyler

Typeset by Avocet Typeset, Chilton, Aylesbury, Bucks

Printing by Bell & Bain Ltd, Scotland

Jim Glazebrook DFC

Contents

FOREWORD
by Keith Jones, Chief Executive, MAF/UK   11

INTRODUCTION
by Bob Swallow   13

AUTHOR'S NOTES and ACKNOWLEDGEMENTS   14

1. EARLY YEARS   17
Childhood memories – Midsomer Norton and
Wallington – My early interest in flying – Christ's
Hospital – My spiritual inheritance – Working for
the Post Office – Start of the war – Battle of Britain –
I get permission to enlist.

2. RAF TRAINING – UK   27
I join the RAF – ACRC Regent's Park – ITW Paignton –
EFTS Elmdon – First solo – Heaton Park Manchester –
SS Montcalm and the Vollendam – Escorts leave us –
Atlantic hazards – Arrival in Canada.

3. OVERSEAS TRAINING – USA   34
Grosse Ile "Elimination Course" – NAS Pensacola –
"Wings" at last! – Aunt Katie's kindness.

4. OVERSEAS TRAINING – CANADA AND THE
   BAHAMAS   50
Back to Canada – I am offered Liberator OTU in the
Bahamas – Make friends with John Johnston – Learning
to fly the Mitchell – Graduate to Liberator – Johnston
and I meet the Duke and Duchess of Windsor.

5.　INTRODUCING 206 SQUADRON　　　　　　63
Return to the UK (after nineteen months) 7 PRC
Harrogate – I meet David Beaty, who takes over my
crew (minus my second pilot) – We learn to fly the
Fortress at Thornaby and Longtown, and are posted
to 206 Squadron – Its distinguished history 1916-1943.

6.　206 SQUADRON IN THE AZORES　　　　　72
The base in the Azores – its crucial role in the Battle of
the Atlantic – Diversion to Santa Anna – U-boat
operations in general – Destruction of U-575.

7.　BACK TO LIBERATORS　　　　　　　　81
Training at Aldergrove – First visit to Glenarm –
St Eval – Operation Cork – Move to Leuchars – Given
a command – Extremes of North Atlantic weather – An
unusually long training flight.

8.　THE LAST MONTHS OF WWII IN EUROPE　　90
Flight Lieutenant Hancock crashes on take off – The
survivors die with Flying Officer Carlisle after relieving
me off the coast of Norway – Flying Officer Frost escapes
attacks by three ME110s – I escape a destroyer's fire,
which badly damages David Beaty's aircraft – I lose
George Ellison.

9.　CONVERSION TO TRANSPORT COMMAND　103
Preparations for transport role – I fly Transport
Command VIPs to Ballykelly, make two return trips
to India and fly empty to Melsbroek to collect army
passengers from NW Europe – My most frightening
take off – I am given job of writing Squadron history –
Its preparation and distribution.

10. THE ORIGINS AND DEVELOPMENT OF MAF   110
Visit of Trevor Strong and Murray Kendon to
Oakington – Early pioneers in missionary aviation –
CAMF and Australian MAF – Harry Hartwig's service
and death – brief outline of growth of MAF

11. OUT OF THE RAF BUT NOT FINISHED WITH
     FLYING   121
I consider the options, return to P.O. telephones – and
get married – Join the RAFVR and Surrey Flying Club –
I am promoted to Manchester – Become MAF's first
honorary representative – Flying with Lancs. Aero Club
then re-commissioned into RAFVR for Air Experience
flying at Woodvale.

12. MY LAST YEARS IN THE TELEPHONE SERVICE   137
Moving to Lancaster – Burton-in-Lonsdale – The link
with Richard Thornton – Retirement.

13. CAMPS, HOLIDAYS AND REUNIONS   143
MAF/Crusader camps – holidays – Kinloss reunions,
and a family one – Someone to watch over me.

POSTSCRIPT from Bob Swallow   153

LIST OF ILLUSTRATIONS   154

BIBLIOGRAPHY   157

INDEX   158

Foreword

I recall first meeting Jim Glazebrook at a conference in Lancashire. It will not surprise the reader to know that the conference was for MAF's volunteer workers. In a sense this is a metaphor that describes much of what Jim stood for – always about the Lord's business and always willing to volunteer his time and services for others.

I am sure that he will forgive me for saying that, like many people, he does not strike you immediately as a dynamic man. But get to know him and you soon begin to realise that, behind that quiet and gentle exterior lies a man of action, single-minded and committed to any God-given task.

Following my first meeting I got to know Jim and his wife Betty very well, enjoying their gracious hospitality in the little village of Burton-in-Lonsdale. Having read Jim's autobiography I am left with a feeling of regret – regret that I had not met him earlier and known him longer, for who would not have wanted to serve under such a man. I see in Jim many of the qualities we read of in Barnabas. He, too, was a man deeply committed to the cause of Christ, never counting the cost of following the Master but always with one eye on the personal needs of others. Always prepared to offer the hand of friendship to those with whom he came into contact.

His story, "Someone to Watch Over Me", says it all and to try and add to it would be to dilute a strong and wonderful testimony of a man whose love for God and commitment to His claim upon his life is so evident. But in a very lovely way Jim's own qualities and character shine through and far from diverting the reader's attention from the Lord, his testimony actually serves to develop our faith in a God who can use such a gentle and caring man in the hostile environment of war without glorifying it.

There is a refreshing honesty and openness to Jim's book, quite prepared to say he was not sure when he found Christ and unafraid to admit defeat. "Falling flat on our faces" is not something we would want too many to know about, but as Jim relates the early days of his walk with the Lord it actually helps the reader. It leaves one thinking, then there is hope for me!

But almost in contrast to his contrition and guilelessness there shines through a tenacity that was clearly an essential ingredient to becoming a successful RAF pilot. How many would, with only a bicycle for transport, work regularly a sixteen-hour day in order to achieve a personal ambition. Then came war and his ambition became a mission – but still at the heart of that mission was the Lord. What reader will not smile at the picture of this young man on his first solo flight so full of enthusiasm singing hymns as he went round his first circuit.

Our paths crossed not long after I joined MAF as a pilot and Jim was a seasoned and very effective speaker on MAF's behalf. Jim, and Betty, played a major part in the success of MAF. They prayed for the work and its workers. They arranged church meetings for those on furlough. They helped in the raising of personal support for the workers as well as general income for the work overseas.

Jim, of course represents many who have volunteered their time, energy and resources to enable the work of MAF to be so successful, and while he would be the first to say that he was only doing what the Lord told him to do, none would disagree that he has been one of our most successful volunteer co-workers.

I commend "Someone to Watch Over Me" not only as an autobiography of a lovely Christian man, but as a devotional book, and one that through Jim's honesty and openness, will serve to draw you closer to the One that watches over each one of us.

Keith Jones
Chief Executive, MAF/UK

Introduction by Bob Swallow

I have known Jim Glazebrook for the greater part of twenty-two years yet still find it difficult to reconcile his flat cap and large shopping bag with many of the exploits recorded here.

Jim is a very modest man who has for many years lived with his wife Betty in Burton-in-Lonsdale, just on the White Rose side of the Lancashire-Yorkshire border. For a large part of his working life he was employed within the Red Rose County. In particular the story focuses on Jim's World War Two experiences, which were in many respects unusual though in others both terrifying and elating.

Jim's story has been recorded with the aid of a tape recorder. On occasions while hammering away at the keyboard transcribing his recollections I have found tears coursing down my cheeks at what he has recounted. There are not too many of his generation left and it is important that we have a lasting record of their triumphs and disasters, good times and bad, before it is too late. My involvement has in reality been simply to jog his memory and act as his pen.

*

As a result of generous gifts to cover the cost of preparation and printing of this book, all profits from the sale of this book will be donated to Mission Aviation Fellowship.

Author's Notes and Acknowledgements

Bob Swallow's claim to have done no more than "jog his memory and act as his pen" does not do justice to his initiative, persistence and sheer hard work in obtaining and transcribing the early drafts of this book. The traumatic events of WWII, coupled with my impressionable age at the time, have undoubtedly left indelible memories – but without Bob's enthusiastic encouragement most of this would never have been recorded.

David Beaty, whose Second Pilot I was for some months in 1943/4, pressed me on a number of occasions to write of my experiences, and even used my account of one incident in a book of his own. His widow, Betty Campbell Beaty, who wrote the brilliant biography of David's life, "Winged Life" (Airlife Publishing, 2001), has given me constant encouragement from the start, patiently reading and commenting helpfully on each draft.

Thain Flowers, who with his wife Jean has been so good to me and Betty during the last few difficult years, has been outstanding with his editorial assistance and patient reproduction of later drafts, and I am grateful too to Glyn Price for all he has done to prepare the work for publication. Thanks also to Helen McGowan and my nephew John Caswell for reading the manuscript and making helpful comments. Richard Roper and Jim Penberthy, the publishers, have a ministry in assisting Christian writers and missions to get their work to the public, and it was a real delight to discover them and to work with them. Andrew Golba of Harvest Fields, our distributor, made the initial contact, and I am very grateful for all his assistance.

My thanks are due to Keith Jones, Chief Executive of MAF/UK for his kind foreword and provision of photographs of MAF work, and I'm grateful to Stuart King for permission to quote from his book "Hope has Wings" (the history of MAF/UK) and to Mrs Margaret Baldock (formerly Hartwig) and MAF/Australia for information on the 50-year celebrations of the latter in Papua New Guinea, and the quote from Vic Ambrose's book "Balus Bilong Mipela" on the origins of MAF in Australia.

Last but not least, I am grateful to my wife Betty for her continual interest in all stages of preparation, and her constant patience through many hours of writing and rewriting.

Chapter 1

Early Years

Scene: A small primary school in Surrey. The windows are set high so that pupils are not distracted. A strict schoolmaster watches to ensure that all eyes are directed to the text being studied.

Suddenly the quiet is disturbed by the sound of two biplane fighters having a mock dog-fight in the sky; the high windows provide exciting glimpses. The master calls sharply for the class to attend to their books, then catches two boys paying furtive glances at the sky. "Go outside and watch the airplanes," he says, "And stay in for half-an-hour's detention after school."

A few minutes later, the two aircraft collide in mid-air. One falls onto an empty house, the other onto a chicken shed at the bottom of a garden. Both pilots parachute to safety.

Needless to say, the errant boys think the spectacle well worth half-an hour's detention, and are the envy of us all.

*

I was born in Teddington, Middlesex, on 11th January 1920, but a few months later my parents moved to Midsomer Norton in Somerset. In the next seven years, we moved within the village, no less than three times.

In the attic of our first home, The Grange, Dad built my first model railway. There was a large clockwork engine to which we had lost the key, so I pushed the train round by hand – but never up the loop line into the bay as once I had seen a movement there – a rat perhaps. I also remember the time my mother caught me sitting up in bed when I was supposed to be asleep, thumbing through the hymn book and singing all the ones I recognised at the top of my voice.

My first day at school coincided with one of the moves, so I was taken to school from one place and to my new home at the end of the day. During the General Strike of 1926, I excitedly rushed into the house shouting "A train, a train", when after days of silence the first two-wagon milk train manned by a volunteer crew came down the track we could see from the garden.

Eventually in Midsomer Norton we stayed with the Vicarage family, and sat in the front pew of the Church. One Sunday, halfway through the morning service, as we were reciting the Creed, my mother noticed I was still wearing my school cap and snatched it from my head. That had tremendous psychological repercussions. For years afterwards, and sometimes even today, I subconsciously run my hand over my head as I walk into church – just to make sure I am uncovered.

That year, 1927, my parents parted company. They did not agree with divorce and re-marriage, and so no legal separation was arranged. By mutual agreement my mother kept my sister, while I went to live with my father and his parents in a house they purchased in Wallington, Surrey. For a time, parts of my school holidays were spent with my mother and sister.

In Wallington I attended the local church school. The incident cited at the beginning of this chapter served to further enhance my interest in flying. My father had always wanted to fly, but never had the opportunity. He built flying models, one of which had a petrol engine, every part of which he constructed himself. Unfortunately its power to weight ratio was not high enough; the best flight it achieved was from the ridge of the house roof for a straight mile during which it gradually lost height.

During our Wallington days I was a frequent visitor to Croydon aerodrome, at that time the main London airport, where I admired the four-engined Imperial Airways biplanes, in addition to many smaller aircraft. On different days during the summer of 1930, I saw big airships, the R100 and the ill-fated R101, sailing majestically overhead. I thought they seemed low, but were probably bigger, and therefore higher than I realised. The highlight of each year was the visit with my father to the Hendon air display. It is a pity that Dad never

Myself, aged 8, at Wallington

lived to see his son become a pilot; he would have been so thrilled. He died of a cerebral haemorrhage, aged forty-three, in 1940.

In 1930, at the age of ten, I was sent to Christ's Hospital, the "Bluecoat School" just outside Horsham. For the first year I was in the Prep, where we were looked after very kindly. One of my principal memories is of our lady teacher reading to us

Myself, aged 10, at Christ's Hospital

in the dormitory each evening, from the recently published "Pooh" books. It made me an A. A. Milne fan for life.

After the special coaching I had received in Wallington before taking the Christ's Hospital entrance exam, I found classroom work easy, ending the year top of the Prep with several prizes. Alas, that was fatal; in following years in the Senior School, I daydreamed my way through class, and exam results suffered as a consequence. At the age of sixteen I sat Matriculation, passing in English, Maths, Advanced Maths, and Engineering Drawing and Design, though failing in German and Chemistry. My House Master wanted me to stay on and sit again in January 1937, but this was not to be.

Sport had an important place in the Christ's Hospital routine, being allocated approximately two hours daily – at the end of

My house – Thornton B, with Swimming Cup and Chess Shield, July 1934 (I am at the extreme right, one row from the back)

afternoon classes in the summer and before them in the winter. We played rugby in the winter terms and also did some cross-country running, both of which I enjoyed. The main summer sport was cricket, at which I was never very good, but there was also swimming. I learned to swim at the age of eleven, and a year or two later found myself a member of the school Swimming Sixteen, where we swam every day and were excused cricket. Voluntary classes to learn the "crawl" proved so popular that all the Swimming Sixteen were trained to act as instructors.

In 1934, my house won the swimming cup and also the chess shield. I was not brilliant at the latter, though did well enough to earn a place on the house team. My only individual sporting prize was for the half-mile swimming race – for which I received an inscribed watch, which was stolen from my clothes while I was enjoying a sea bathe during the summer holidays!

The charter of Christ's Hospital proclaims it to be a

"Religious, Royal and Ancient Foundation". We had a service in the school chapel every morning, twice on Sundays. I do not recall any resentment at this being felt or expressed by anyone. We took it for granted as part of the accepted routine. Neither was I conscious of any particular spiritual uplift. There must have been some benefit from hearing the Bible read and I always enjoyed a good sing. We had a particularly enthusiastic musical director in Dr C.S. Lang, a cousin of the former Archbishop of Canterbury, who trained the whole school in singing. He arranged for the London Symphony Orchestra to give a concert at the school annually, and prepared us beforehand to appreciate each piece in the programme.

Sermons were invariably given over to daydreaming. I do not recall ever being challenged by one in a personal way. I did however attend the Christian Union which met in a classroom

Thornton B Swimmers, July 1934, with Swimming Cup. (I am at the extreme right, centre row).

after chapel on Sunday mornings, being addressed by a variety of visiting speakers, many of them Old Blues, as former pupils of Christ's Hospital are called. Many of these speakers did have challenging things to say. It was here and also at the Wallington Crusaders' Bible Class, which I attended on Sunday afternoons during the school holidays, that I made my first response to the Gospel. There were well over 200 boys at Crusaders, and the Senior Leader, Mr H.V. Hedderly, shook hands with each of us as we arrived, and after leading the Class, marked up the register from memory after he got home. He was a great man of prayer, and few of us realised till much later (if at all) how much we owe to his caring and prayerful concern for each one of us.

I believe it was John Stott who pointed out that we should not know our physical birthdays if our parents had not told us, adding that many of us will not know our spiritual birthday until our heavenly Father tells us when we arrive in Heaven. I do not recall any Gospel appeal to which I did not respond in my heart, yet there was no dramatic moment of decision as such. I have never doubted the existence of God and have always wanted to serve Him. Yet, I was a defeated Christian for so long, falling flat on my face again and again. It was not until it dawned on me, years later, that no matter how many times I fell, there was no question of giving up, that my faith began to mature.

It was many years later that I became aware of a unique spiritual inheritance. John William Fletcher (1729-1785), "Fletcher of Madeley" as he is generally known from the scene of his labours, was most saintly – and the one of all men whom John Wesley admired and respected most. Wesley found in him the fullest realisation of what he meant by Christian perfection. His noble funeral sermon on the Vicar of Madeley, from the suggestive text, "Mark the perfect man, and behold the upright, for the end of that man is peace", is the strongest and most unqualified eulogy he ever uttered. Fletcher was thoroughly worthy of this admiration, for a more Christlike man never lived. It is said that Voltaire, when challenged to produce a character as perfect as that of our Lord, at once mentioned Fletcher of Madeley.

In 1760 when John Fletcher arrived to commence his ministry, one 16-year old Madeley lad was so influenced by his godly vicar that he was led to the ministry himself, thus becoming the Rev. James Glazebrook. He was my great-great-great grandfather. The word of God warns us of the inevitable consequences of sin, reaching even to "the third and fourth generation", but promises mercy and love "to a thousand generations of those who love (God) and keep his commandments". I count myself privileged therefore to share a little of this spiritual heritage from merely five generations back!

With my interest in flying having been aroused early, I hung on every word when a team of RAF officers visited the school to encourage recruitment. An interview resulted in an assurance that, subject to my medical fitness, I should be accepted into the RAF on a Short Service Commission. However, my father though sympathetic to my desire to fly was cautious. Having experienced the unemployment trauma of the early thirties, he was anxious to see me settled into permanent employment and regarded a Short Service Commission as rather a dead-end.

He would have encouraged me to go in for Civil Aviation, but that was a costly venture, and consequently, he sought advice about careers within the Post Office Telephone Service. I could have stayed on at school until I was nineteen but the Post Office said they would rather have me with three years' experience in their department than with three more years of general education. So, after an interview, I left Christ's Hospital in mid-term on 29th October 1936, reporting two days later to the Croydon Telephone Exchange to commence as a "Youth in Training", i.e. an engineering apprentice. I looked with awe at the SW1 (Skilled Workman Class 1) who told me he had been with the Post Office for thirty years.

The thought of flying was not, however, abandoned. I enquired about the Royal Air Force Volunteer Reserve, which was prepared to train recruits from scratch. In addition to weekend activities, they required attendance at evening classes three times a week. Unfortunately, so too did the Post Office if I wished to obtain the technical qualifications to progress in my new career. My father in his wisdom persuaded me that the latter must have priority. I might take up flying when my career training was over.

Looking back I wonder how I stuck a job in which the hours of work were from 8 a.m. to 5.45 p.m. I left home at 7 a.m. cycling an hour to work, and having a few sandwiches for tea before pedalling a fair distance to the evening class which began at 7 p.m. and ended around three hours later. A further ride took me home which was reached around eleven. This was on three nights a week, homework occupying another two.

In 1938 there was a scare over what was referred to as the Czechoslovakian Affair when that country was in effect handed to Hitler in an act of appeasement. The reserve forces were hurriedly called up, and as the telephone service had encouraged its staff to join the territorial forces, it lost half its engineers overnight, mostly into the Royal Corps of Signals. An embargo was placed on further personnel volunteering, even when war broke out in 1939. Shortly before that I helped to install switchboards in country houses outside London where banks and insurance companies planned to move their staff to escape the expected bombing of the capital.

On Friday, 1st September 1939, the day on which German troops marched into Poland, we started on just such a switchboard in a country house in Surrey. Word arrived that we were to stay on the job until it was finished. We worked through Friday and the following night, all day Saturday until the early evening, at which point the foreman said to me, "You're only a lad, go home and get a night's sleep and come back tomorrow". The rest of the team worked through a second night, the switchboard being finished by 6 p.m. Sunday evening. For six or seven weeks we worked a seven-day week, twelve to fourteen hours per day.

Later I was transferred back to maintenance work at the Telephone Exchange at Mitcham. Those were the days before long distance dialling, and the majority of calls other than local ones had to be connected by an operator. Some fifty or more operators were employed at the Mitcham exchange, working at a switchboard situated on the top floor of the building. This was not the healthiest spot when bombs were falling, and a small switchboard was installed in the basement, where emergency circuits were connected and which served also as an air raid shelter, being strengthened with concrete beams.

When the bombing raids started in 1940, it was too disruptive to evacuate the switchboard every time there was an air raid warning as there might be several such each day without the exchange itself being in any real danger. So an alarm bell was installed on the roof. Being the one member of staff who could tell one type of aircraft from another I was appointed to go to the roof every time we had a warning. If I saw bombers approaching, I sounded the alarm, whereupon the supervisors would marshal the operators down to the shelter, while the other engineers came up with me to the roof to watch the action!

At the end of 1940, after the Battle of Britain in which we lost large numbers of aircrew, an appeal went out for pilots and navigators. My long-term desire to fly had been heightened by the Battle of Britain, much of which I observed from ground level, so I wrote to Post Office HQ requesting permission to enlist. A decree followed that anyone wishing to train, either as pilot or navigator – but no others, as we were in a reserved occupation – would be allowed to volunteer. Early in 1941, four of us from the same telephone exchange enrolled on the same day.

All of us became pilots. The other three failed to return from operations.

Chapter 2

RAF Training – UK

In May 1941 I was called to one of the Oxford colleges to take psychological, medical and physical tests. After three days I was given a number and rank, sworn in and with the rest of the successful applicants sent back to our civilian jobs to await call-up. Since 1938 I had been an Assistant Leader of the Wallington Crusader Class and it was quite a wrench to leave all that behind when I was finally called up during August 1941. Crusader Fellowship discussions had of course covered the Christian attitude to war, among many other subjects. My feeling was with those who considered that war was, and always had been, judgement; only those who could say that their own sin had not contributed to this judgement had the right to opt out of the consequences. But some of my friends were conscientious objectors. One, who was at school with me, did very dangerous bomb disposal work during the London blitz, subsequently volunteering for the airborne RAMC. He was dropped by parachute during the Normandy landings in 1944 in the wrong place, spending the rest of the war as a prisoner of the Germans. Once, after the war, travelling with him to a meeting in London, I stepped off the bus as it slowed for the corner outside the meeting place. Jack carried on another hundred yards to the official bus stop before walking back to join me. When I asked him why he didn't do as I had done, he replied, "Not me, I've had enough of jumping out of moving vehicles!"

On the 18th August 1941 I reported to St John's Wood on the edge of Regent's Park, London, where we were billeted in flats that were completed just prior to the outbreak of war and were as yet unoccupied. Meals were taken in the zoo restaurant. We were marched here and there, kitted out, lectured, injected and vaccinated against who knows what? Our limited resources allowed the occasional supper in a Lyon's Corner House, and twice-weekly visits to the News Theatre, where the programme changed on Mondays and Thursdays, servicemen in uniform being admitted for 4d (four old pennies).

After three weeks we split into groups, my group being sent to No 4 Initial Training Wing in Paignton, South Devon, for lectures on theory of flight, aircraft recognition, airmanship, airframes, engines, meteorology and many other subjects. Additionally for two months we endured at least two hours' drill and PT per day. If we worked well at these we were allowed a fifteen-minute sea bathe to round off the period. Never was I so fit, either before or since. The weather that autumn was superb.

We were billeted in a requisitioned hotel, the Tembani, on the Marine Parade. Four of us shared what had once been a single room. Daily inspections ensured that our belongings, kit and bedding were kept in order, the bare boards of the floor having to be scrubbed every weekend in our "free time". Fortunately for me, one of the others shared my objections to unnecessary Sunday work, so by agreement with the remainder, he and I scrubbed the boards every other Saturday, the others doing so on the alternate Sundays.

On 1st November, 1941, together with six other members of our group, I arrived at No. 14 Elementary Flying Training School at Elmdon, now better known as Birmingham International Airport. If you pass it in the train, you can still see the original administration building complete with a projecting roof canopy. While I was there a flyer who remained nameless dived in a Hurricane from a great height and flew beneath the canopy. Had anyone in authority caught his number he would surely have been for the high jump. Like many others

Part of the Course No. 30, No. 14 EFTS, Elmdon, November 1941 (showing all seven RAF trainees – I am extreme left – there were 49 FAA Cadets in all)

With my first Instructor, P/O Andrews, Elmdon, November 1941

our introduction to flying was to be in the Tiger Moth, a two-seater open cockpit biplane. Pilot Officer Andrews, my instructor on the Tiger Moth, though eighteen months my junior, had four hundred hours' experience of flying this aircraft to the exclusion of all other types. He could do anything with a Tiger Moth, sometimes returning from an exercise doing slow rolls all the way. The pupil sat in the back, the instructor in front. The front seat was over the centre of gravity so it didn't affect the balance of the aircraft whether it was occupied or not. It was not possible to fly it solo from the front seat without additional ballast behind.

My first flight with PO Andrews was on 3rd November, a gentle twenty-minute exercise entitled "Air experience and familiarity with cockpit layout". A short fifteen days later, after nine more trips and with six-and-a-quarter hours' flying time beneath my belt, I completed my first solo, for every pilot a never-to-be-forgotten moment. Sitting in the open rear cockpit, wearing leather gauntlets, helmet and goggles, and with the empty cockpit in front emphasising that I really was in the air

Tiger Moth T 7222 – My first solo, 18 November 1941

alone, I flew round the circuit, banging the outside of the air-craft singing "Praise my Soul the King of Heaven" at the top of my voice!

At Elmdon during a wet month, much of the airfield was waterlogged. A Walrus amphibian aircraft attempting to make a landing in these conditions, circled several times before touching down in a sea of spray. Wagers had been made as to whether the pilot would land with his wheels up or down!

On our course, there were only seven RAF trainees, all the rest being Fleet Air Arm cadets. My theory was that a minimum number of RAF personnel were on each course in order that the station did not have to be handed over to the Navy. Training continued until mid-December when, without notice, four of the seven, myself included, were called into the office, given a fortnight's embarkation leave and told to report to Heaton Park, Manchester, on Boxing Day 1941. By now I had almost thirty hours' flying time.

During the war many thousands of RAF aircrew were sent overseas for the greater part of their training. On the one hand, the UK was fully occupied with operational requirements, and on the other it provided an opportunity for the Commonwealth nations, particularly Canada, Rhodesia and South Africa, to make a positive contribution to our war effort. America, too, helped – even before they were drawn into the conflict by the dastardly Japanese attack at Pearl Harbour.

After ten days of lectures and inoculations at Heaton Park, Manchester, we were sent overnight by train to Gourock on the Clyde to board what had once been a 20000 ton Dutch luxury liner, the Montcalm. How many thousand were packed into this troopship is anyone's guess. Several hundred of us were billeted in the former ballroom. When all the sleeping bags were unrolled there was simply no floor space left. There was barely room to walk anywhere.

We set sail next morning into the Irish Sea for the short haul to Pembroke Dock in West Wales where we joined the

"Vollendam", another liner of about the same size. Putting out into the Atlantic we had two destroyers as escort. The weather worsened. One of the destroyers way out to starboard started to signal in plain language by lamp. Lamp signalling in morse was something we had already learned. So we read, "cannot maintain speed without suffering damage". The result was that we reduced speed until darkness fell, when the destroyers turned back. We were now on our own.

These two passenger liners would no doubt have been stable when steaming in a straight line, but because a U-boat crew would need seven-and-a-half minutes to get an accurate measure of speed and direction of a potential victim, every seven minutes we changed course at speed through sixty degrees. The liner heeled over, taking the greater part of the following seven minutes to recover its former poise before the process was repeated. As luxury liners, steaming a straight course, they would have been comfortable boats, yet with the continual rolling nearly everyone was sick. After two days I began to feel better.

By now it was 11th January 1942 and my birthday, memorable also because I was selected for twenty-four hours of guard duty, two hours on duty at a given point followed by two off in the guardroom somewhere in the bowels of the ship. My duty point was immediately above the galley and I was continually retching trying to be sick, with no sympathy from anyone. It upset my digestion so badly that I never ate a proper meal during the rest of the voyage. Ken Graves, a member of our group who had been with us at Paignton, brought an apple up to me on deck from time to time. That was one of the few items of food my digestive system managed to keep down. It was three weeks after our arrival in Canada before I had fully recovered my appetite.

With many variations in course, it took sixteen days to cross the Atlantic. Clearly the captain received information as to where U-boats were thought to be lurking as one day we appeared to be in near-Arctic regions and three days later the conditions were almost tropical. Just before arriving in Canada, we ran into a hurricane and for two days sat head into wind, the sea being a maelstrom of boiling water. It was impossible to see more than 100 yards. It transpired that where we should have been, had not the hurricane upset arrangements, two ships were torpedoed.

We arrived at Halifax, Nova Scotia, on 19th January. Not being expected, we lay in the harbour for a further twenty-four hours while arrangements were made for our handling. Once ashore, we were put on a train, my first impression being the enormous size of the steam engine and carriages compared to their British equivalents. A journey that took several hours ended at a reception centre in Moncton, New Brunswick. The centre was known as No.31 Personnel Depot and here we stayed for six weeks. On the first Sunday three or four of us went into town to the evening church service, after which we were inundated with invitations to spend evenings with local families, much to the chagrin of our non-churchgoing mates, who asked: "Have you been here before?"

It was at Moncton that we first learned that we were destined for Coastal Command, and would be trained by the United States Navy at their big air base in Pensacola, Florida, on the coast of the Gulf of Mexico. In all, some 4000 British airmen were trained there. Once more we were to be accompanied by cadets from the Fleet Air Arm, who would complete their training on carrier-borne aircraft. We RAF types were destined to end up on flying boats.

Chapter 3

Overseas Training – USA

On 2nd March a group of us set off, by train again, on a two-day journey through Canada via Montreal, Toronto and Windsor, Ontario, and then into the USA at Detroit. Our destination was the U.S. Naval Reserve Air Base on Grosse Ile in the Detroit River. The island was joined to the mainland by a bridge, though as befits a naval unit one might only go "ashore" in the "liberty boat" – a bus! Here there was an airfield where the US Navy ran what they referred to quite bluntly as an "Elimination Course" designed to "eliminate" those whom our instructors decided would not make successful pilots. We flew only until being given a "first solo". The fact that we had done any flying before was completely ignored. The deal that had been struck with the RAF and Fleet Air Arm was that we should be trained exactly as if we were members of the US forces. This sounded reasonable until one remembered that Britain was engaged in a struggle to survive and was desperately short of pilots, while the Americans had virtually unlimited supplies of men and money.

Trainee pilots could be failed for a variety of reasons, not only performance in the air, and many of my colleagues who could fly as well as I were sent back to Canada to retrain as navigators. Another shock was our introduction to US Navy discipline. In the British forces, the only essential requirement was to be present on the first parade of the day, washed, shaved and properly dressed. If you want to have a lie in and miss your breakfast, that's your look-out! In the US Navy, "reveille" has the status of a parade. The bell rang at 4.45 am (horrors!) the duty officer following thirty seconds later. Anyone who did not have his "feet on the deck" was on a charge! This early call was followed by PT from 5.00 to 5.20 am; breakfast started at a quarter to six and work – whether lectures or flying – began at 7.00 am. Later, when we continued our training in the tropical heat of Florida, this early schedule made sense. We had a three-hour break during the hottest part of the day, then flew again until the evening.

Naval Aircraft N3N – the "Yellow Peril"

The US Navy's primary trainer was, like the Tiger Moth, a two-seater open cockpit biplane, but twice as heavy and three times as powerful. Its official designation was the N3N – and from its colour it was known colloquially as the "Yellow Peril". The Tiger Moth had been an excellent introduction to flying. You would have a job to kill yourself in it though it was tricky to land being so light. The basic premise on landing is to level off and let the speed drop until you fall out of the air. Being so light if you were more than six inches above ground the Tiger

Moth bounced all over the place. It was a safe plane to fly but difficult to fly well. The N3N on the other hand was much more solid. You could stall it three feet up and it just landed heavily without bouncing.

While at Grosse Ile, I suffered a recurrence of tonsillitis, an affliction which had beset me before more than once. I was carted off to the US Navy hospital and there pumped full of Sulphanilamide, at that time an experimental drug. This reduced my temperature but left me more ill from its side effects. Consequently, although I had been sent solo on 19th March, I slipped a course before going on to the next stage of training at the end of April.

Those of us who survived the "elimination course" next took a three-day train journey to Pensacola via Toledo, Cincinnati, (Ohio), Louisville, Nashville (Kentucky), Birmingham and Montgomery (Alabama). Here, in my case for the third time, we were treated as though we had just arrived off the street having six weeks of ground school before "initial instruction" and then going solo for a third time, again in the N3N. That was on 2nd July 1942. I was seriously wondering whether I should ever get into the war in Europe. My qualms were to prove groundless, though it was by now mid-1942 and I had requested permission to join up at the end of 1940. The Yanks were in no hurry and were inclined to throw anyone off the course for the slightest misdemeanour. A good friend whom I regarded as a far better pilot than myself, on returning from a solo exercise, landed safely and well before taxiing round a row of parked aircraft. Whether he was caught by a gust of wind or simply misjudged his position I shall never know. He touched wingtips with the end plane and that was that. Any taxiing accident was the pilot's fault. He went straight back to Canada. It was tragic really. Of our original course, only one third obtained their pilot's wings.

I had another attack of tonsillitis during our ground school course but was terrified to go sick, as my course was to be the

Myself at Pensacola, June 1942

Building 624, the British Flight Battalion accommodation, Pensacola

last of this nature. Future courses would be conducted at Grosse Ile. Now in the hot climate of this part of America they had public water fountains situated in every corridor. I confided in my lecturer my problem and he permitted me to slip out every quarter of an hour or so to gargle with strong salt water. I kept this up for three days finally curing the tonsillitis for good without having to report sick. And it never recurred.

Pensacola was an enormous base, manned by 20,000 people

and with five main airfields and forty satellite fields having 2,000 aircraft in the air on any normal working day. Before our first flight we had to pass a written exam on the routes we needed to take just taxiing around the airfields.

Flying-wise they had a testing system involving an independent instructor who had never flown with the trainee before. Nor had he seen his record or communicated with the man's own instructor. The first tests took place after twenty and thirty-three hours' flying time, respectively. If you failed a test, all was not lost. Next day you might have a further attempt with a different instructor. The ethos was that you needed to pass twice out of a maximum three attempts. Even then if, say, you had two failures and one pass, your case would go before a board where you might, after representation by your own instructor, be allowed a further period of extra training. Then two "ups" had to be obtained. I had to jump through this particular hoop twice, eventually succeeding with a pass, failure and a final pass at the sixth attempt. My last test instructor had a reputation for downing British students, which did little to help my morale that morning and might well have seen a premature end to my flying career. I went through agonies and prayed harder than ever before.

One of the exercises flying the N3N in the twenty-hour check was a practice forced landing in a circle painted in a field. The ritual was to fly downwind at 1000 feet, cut the throttle, making a controlled glide through an S-turn prior to completing a fully stalled landing in the circle. You had to complete this to the satisfaction of independent scrutiny six times out of seven. As soon as you had touched down, you opened up again as there were others following behind, possibly nine or ten aircraft doing circuits and bumps. To start with you dropped off your instructor further out in the field, all your colleagues doing likewise. The group of instructors would sit down playing crap (a gambling game using two dice), just one keeping an eye and passing comment on the participants circling and landing.

During my period of extra time my instructor, bless him, taught me a useful trick. It amounted to this. If I was coming in high, I should pull the nose up, thus causing the speed to drop when descent would be more rapid. Conversely, if I was too low, and in this hot climate I might dive towards the ground, obtain extra lift from the cushion of humid air and glide a little further. An inexperienced student would never have thought of this.

I employed these tactics to good effect on my final (6th) check. My first approach seemed high, so I pulled the nose up and dropped steeply, just managing to get into the far edge of the circle. Though I tried to correct for this, my second approach was still a little high, but I managed to drop into the centre of the circle. As I began my third circuit, I thought to myself, "whatever happens I must show that I know what I am doing – I mustn't be high three times running". So I over-corrected and found myself low on the approach. Using the dodge I had been taught I just managed to stagger into the near edge

"S-turns to Circles" – the circle we had to land in taken from 1000 feet, the point of engine cut

of the circle. At this point the check pilot leaped to his feet and signalled me to come in. My immediate reaction was that he was going to fail me for doing these tricks, and my heart was in my boots for the five minutes it took me to fly round the circuit and land on the designated portion of the field. "Done this before, haven't you?", he demanded. He climbed in, and we proceeded with the rest of the check, after which to my great relief he gave me the thumbs up. Thankfully I never suffered another 'down' in the rest of my training.

We moved on to the Stearman, a somewhat more advanced biplane. In some respects it glided like a brick compared to the N3N. We practised aerobatics and formation flying. Then it was onto a monoplane, the Harvard, which we flew by instruments under a hood, never seeing the ground. An instructor occupied the rear seat. The Harvard was very sensitive to the controls. We used to say that if you wanted to do a gentle (rate half) turn, all you needed to do was to think about it and the reflex action of your muscles would result in sufficient movement of the controls for the plane to complete the manoeuvre!

Our next aircraft was a land-based version of the Kingfisher, a type built initially as a seaplane. It weighed in the order of ten tons, which was large for a single-engined plane. The dual control was inefficient, a tiny joystick and rudder bar being located in the rear cockpit for the instructor. Apart from the initial check, we flew solo and practised more formation flying in either three- or nine-plane formations. Although we had radios, pupils were not allowed to transmit other than in an emergency. One time an instructor jawed away interminably until at length a very English voice broke in with "How about some peace and quiet?" The culprit was never found.

Now we moved on to the flying boats, spending four or five hours in the Sesqui-plane, a strange one-and-a-half-wing beast, before graduating to the Catalina. This was a fair-sized reconnaissance aircraft, twin-engined with a crew of up to eight or even ten. Some long range squadrons flew Catalina patrols of

Three-plane formation – N3Ns

Three-plane formation – Kingfishers

If you look carefully, there are two planes in each of these photographs, one almost unseen behind the other. The third plane of the formation is the one from which the photo is taken.

Consolidated Catalina – PBY

Consolidated Sesqui-plane – P2Y

up to twenty-seven hours. Both the Sesqui-plane and the Catalina were Consolidated aircraft. The former was designated P2Y, the latter PBY. My logbook records that the flying boat types which I flew were P2Y-2 and P2Y-3, and Catalina PBY-2, PBY-5 and PBY-5B. The PBY-5A was an amphibian, and I also saw these at Pensacola, though as far as I know no British students flew them. They could be let down the ramp into the sea on their own wheels and, when returning from a flight, could lower their wheels in the water, and motor up the ramp under their own power.

There was one occasion when, pausing to watch a take-off

Initial rush of water as throttles are opened.

Wake narrows as we get "on the step"

End of wake shows point at which we're airborne

Waterborne again

"Circuits and Splashes"

from the water, I wondered why it was taking so long, until to my amazement the plane staggered into the air with its wheels still down! I don't know who was flying it – whether student or instructor – but I wondered if the wheel assembly would have been damaged after being dragged through the water at speed. The incident was not discussed in my hearing, so I never heard the end of that story.

Landing a flying boat involves a different technique from that of a land-based aircraft. It's a matter of flying the machine onto the water rather than stalling. In still water conditions, it is impossible to judge height above water and an instrument landing is necessary. No flying boat was designed for the open sea, always requiring sheltered water. There were of course times when flying boats did land in open sea to rescue people, sometimes they got away with it, on others the plane broke up. After around thirty hours on flying boats, I qualified, and received the official declaration:

Sergeant Pilot John V. Glazebrook has completed the course of training and has met successfully the requirements of the course as prescribed for Naval Aviators of the United States Navy.

This certificate was dated 25 November 1942, and with it I received the brass US Navy's pilots 'wings'. Later as a formality, I was to be presented with RAF wings.

At Pensacola we were normally free on Saturday afternoons and Sundays, though one Saturday afternoon as a punishment for slovenliness on the parade ground we were sentenced to do drill for two hours, organised by one of our number, a former drill sergeant who was transferring to aircrew. He had us performing efficiently – and enjoying it – within the first hour. American students who gathered round the parade ground watched our performance open-mouthed!

On Sundays, breakfast was still at 5.45 am, if we wanted it. Most didn't. A dozen of us bussed into town and breakfasted in

United States Naval Air Station
Pensacola, Florida

Know all men by these presents that

Sergeant Pilot John D. Glazebrook, Royal Air Force

has completed the course of training and has met successfully the requirements of the course as prescribed for

Naval Aviators of the United States Navy

In Witness Whereof, this certificate has been signed on this 25th day of November 19 42 and the Seal of the Naval Air Station hereunto affixed

Commander, U. S. Navy
Superintendent of Aviation Training

Captain, U. S. Navy
Commandant, Naval Air Training Center

US Navy Pilot's qualification certificate, Nov. 1942

a drug-store before attending the morning service at the 1st Presbyterian Church in Pensacola. The minister, Dr Thomas, was a kindly Scot. Many of the congregation entertained us to meals in their homes.

Kathlyn Monroe, a school-teacher who ran the young people's work at the Church, collected details of our next of kin, ostensibly so that she could write if anything happened to us. We discovered that she wrote anyway, to tell our families that we were well and behaving ourselves. Our course ending in November, no one knew where we would be spending Christmas, so Miss Monroe laid on a slap-up Christmas dinner for us on the last Sunday before we left Pensacola.

Subsequently, Aunt Katie, as we called her, kept in touch by Christmas letter for many years. One year she wrote that she had given up teaching, albeit reluctantly, because the State Education authority would not allow her to continue beyond the age of seventy! She retired on a pension of 2% of her salary

Aunt Katie and guests, last Sunday at Pensacola

Miss Kathlyn Monroe (Aunt Katie), June 1942

for every year of service, with no upper limit. So, having taught in the same school for forty-eight years, her pension was 96% of her finishing salary.

During the next two years she suffered ill health, was in hospital for an operation and then, suddenly, she was well enough to visit us. According to her own story, she was waited on by a deputation of her old scholars, with a bag full of travel brochures, and the words, "Miss Monroe, we'd like to send you to Rome". She had taught Latin for years and they imagined that Rome would represent the height of her ambition. Her reply, in her own words as related to us was, "I don't want to go to Rome, I want to go to Britain to see my boys".

That's how much she cared. She hadn't seen us for thirty years, had never met our wives, had never been out of the

United States – yet we were "her boys" still, and she wanted to come and see how each of us had turned out. Her visit lasted three weeks. She stayed in the homes of seven of us and met another three. She visited us on a Friday evening, after quite a long drive and I asked rather tentatively whether she would like a trip out the next day, or was she too tired? She replied that she had come to see people not places, but what had I in mind? Not knowing if someone who had spent all her life in Florida had even heard of the English Lakes, I suggested it. Her eyes lit up: she exclaimed "The Lake District! You couldn't have suggested anything better. I was brought up on Wordsworth!"

And a lovely day out we had, too, before she went on to stay with the next of her boys that she had known and had loved for so long.

Sadly she died before the reunion which my wife Betty and I enjoyed in Pensacola in 1982 when more than a hundred "British Pensacola Veterans" returned to celebrate the fortieth anniversary of our training there.

Memorial to Kathlyn Monroe, 1st Presbyterian Church, Pensacola (1981)

Sergeant Pilot Jim Glazebrook,
November 1942

Sergeant Pilot Ken Graves,
November 1942

The Instructors, Pensacola Flying Boat Squadron

Chapter 4

Overseas Training – Canada and the Bahamas

I was now a qualified pilot, but, alas, not finished with training. After the long train journey back to Canada, we arrived at Moncton again. We spent just a few weeks there, including a week's leave, which I and a friend Leslie Jones spent in Toronto with a family who had offered hospitality to British forces' personnel. Then we set off again, this time on a ferry, which had to break the ice on the frozen St. Lawrence River, eventually arriving at the RAF station at Charlottetown, on Prince Edward Island.

In the early part of the war, the Coastal Command flying boat squadrons did not have separate navigators. A flying boat on patrol would have three pilots, one of which in turn would act as navigator, so we now also had to qualify as navigators. On Prince Edward Island I learned navigation aboard the Mark 1 Anson, the under-carriage of which had to be wound up by hand. This chore always fell to the student, a hundred-and-nineteen turns, as I remember. A month's course sufficed to qualify but then came a snag. We were told there were no immediate flying boat postings. If we wished to stay with flying boats, we could go back to the UK and wait for a posting. (We had already waited two years!) Alternatively, the top ten from the examination results would be given the opportunity to go to the Bahamas to do operational training on Liberators. This was by now April 1943. While Britain had its back to the

John and Jim leaving Moncton, April 1943

I am dwarfed by the engine that pulled us to New York

John, on the engine that pulled us to New York

wall, fighting for its very existence, I headed for the sunny Bahamas with very mixed feelings!

On route to the Bahamas, largely by train, I made friends with my future navigator, John Johnston, an Irishman, son of the Bank Manager in Glenarm, County Antrim. We had decided by the time we arrived in Miami that we would fly together if we could. We had a 24-hour wait in Miami, and spent much of it "window shopping". We were still on an aircraftsman's pay in those days, and had little spare cash. John came from a very musical family, and gazed intently at a clarinet, priced at 24 Dollars (which seemed a vast sum to me) in the window of a second-hand music shop saying, "I've always wanted to play a clarinet". We pooled our last dollars to buy it for him. I thought the purchase very foolish, little knowing

B25 – Mitchell

that John was destined to become an outstanding clarinettist who would play in all three Northern Ireland orchestras. To this day I never hear the Mozart Clarinet Concerto without recollecting John's hours of practice in the ablutions hut in the Bahamas. (The only place he could go without disturbing anybody!)

It was a twenty-four hour journey from Miami to the islands in a flat-bottomed river boat not designed for the open sea. Once more I was plagued by seasickness, being mighty glad not to have joined the Navy.

In the Bahamas we flew Mitchells for a couple of months before moving onto the Liberator. During the first month everybody was doing their own thing as navigators, wireless operators, gunners or pilots. We had been told that we might join up with friends to form our own crews. There was just one imponderable. There were twenty-four pilots for twelve crews, two to each, first and second pilots. We should not know until the end of the first month when assessments had been completed who would be first or second pilots.

The Wing Commander Flying was a bit of a snooty character making it abundantly clear that he disapproved of NCO pilots

Avro Anson over the frozen St Lawrence River, January 1943

Avro Anson flight deck

My first crew – Back row: Draper, Meaker, MacManus, McCrostie and Clegg;
Front row: Johnston, Glazebrook and Simpkin

My first crew – Fred, self and John

on what was the only four-engined Operational Training Unit. We had twenty officers plus just four sergeant pilots. In Pensacola they had an allocation of seven commissions for each course but all who had been in a university air squadron or were ground crew NCOs transferring to aircrew got commissions, so the rest of us were automatically sergeant pilots.

Needless to say, we four sergeants were convinced that we should all be second pilots. John and I teamed up with a Flight Lieutenant, a decent chap and a little older than we were with more flying hours having spent three years in Canada as a staff pilot. I hit it off well with him and we had it all set up that he would be captain, myself second pilot, and John navigator. We made friends with a radio operator and gunners to form a complete crew and were all set to go until they posted the list at the end of the first month. I was down as a Captain.

Our Flight Lieutenant was also appointed a Captain and took our pre-arranged crew other than John, who opted to stay with me. He and I had to make up the rest of our crew from those who had not already arranged who to fly with. In fact, we picked up two Canadian gunners who were later court-martialled for being drunk when they should have been night flying. The full complement of our crew was seven.

One of our first training flights together on a Mitchell was a night navigation exercise over the sea, dark night, no moon, no stars. For the first time, I experienced something that we had all been warned about, but is still difficult to comprehend when it happens. It was always drilled into us that you must never trust your feelings but rely at all times on your instruments. (It was not really known why pilots were so affected until some research was done into it after the war; this revealed the effect of turning on the sensing hairs in the canals of the inner ear.) The other thing instilled into us when night flying was to do gentle rather than steep turns.

Well, we flew out so far and then performed a long slow turn to the left of around one hundred degrees. As soon as I levelled

John and I dressed up to meet the Duke and Duchess of Windsor

Sir Walter Moore, Deputy Governor of the Bahamas

B24 – Liberator

Liberator instrument panel

out my artificial horizon told me I was flying straight and level but I was so sure that we were diving to the right that I thought the artificial horizon had packed up, so I tried to pull out causing the nose of the aircraft to go up to the left. Fortunately, the discipline of our training saved the day; apart from two hundred hours flying I had spent almost one hundred more on the Link trainer, the precursor of today's flight simulator. I reasoned that even if the artificial horizon had packed up, I should check the other instruments, e.g. the airspeed indicator and the rate of climb. From these I was able to tell what was happening and force myself to take corrective action. Three times, after each long turn, I experienced this same phenomenon eventually arriving back safely, albeit somewhat shakily.

The Flight Lieutenant to whom I had anticipated being second pilot crashed into the sea that night. He and all his crew were killed. There was no proof as to what was the cause of the accident though he had carried out, as already mentioned, three years' staff piloting in Canada (most, if not all, in daylight) and I reckon that sadly he was out of touch with instrument flying, had a similar experience to mine and could not cope. John, my navigator, effectively saved his own life by staying loyal to me. All this taught me a lesson – the hard way.

The Mitchell was a wonderful plane to fly though far faster than anything I was used to, landing at around 130 mph as compared to a flying boat at about 60 mph. Again the Mitchell cruised at around 275 to 300 mph, a flying boat by comparison at about 95 mph. Quite frightening really.

Our exercises in the Mitchell included a number of operational patrols, carrying full armament including depth charges, since U-boats were occasionally operating on that side of the Atlantic. I carried out five operational anti-submarine patrols in the Mitchell and another later in a Liberator.

In the O.T.C. at Christ's Hospital, I had become a first-class shot with a rifle, but never seemed to get the hang of aiming a shotgun with both eyes open against a small moving target.

One of the peripheral training activities at Nassau was Clay Pigeon shooting. At the end of one Friday afternoon session of this caper, the officer in charge said; "We have a little time left and enough skeets for three shots each. Lets have a competition putting in a shilling each, winner takes all."

My heart sank. I had always avoided anything resembling gambling, even the apparently innocent raffle. But if I said I didn't want to take part, everyone would think it was because I knew I was a rotten shot and could not win, so I took the easy way out and threw in my shilling with the rest. When my turn came to take the first shot, I scored a direct hit. Oh well, I thought, that was a fluke, it couldn't happen again – but it did! When it came to the third shot I actually tried to miss, but hit the skeet again! Everyone was amazed – and twenty-nine shillings burnt a hole in my pocket until I put them in the collection plate on Sunday.

That was in the Methodist church in Nassau, which John Johnston and I attended together whenever we were free to do so. The minister was a retired missionary and his sermons were quite exceptional. Our contact with this church was to prove memorable in two unexpected ways.

Sir Walter Moore, Deputy Governor of the Bahamas, had some connection with the Methodist church, and let it be known that servicemen attending there were invited to make use of his tennis court, the only grass court on the island. John and I took advantage of this, and, with several others went up to play from time to time. One evening when we were there, Sir Walter came out to speak to us, saying that on the following Wednesday he would be entertaining the Duke and Duchess of Windsor to dinner, and if we were there he would present us to them. So John and I put on our cleanest uniforms for the occasion and were in due course presented to the Duke and Duchess, who chatted to us very amicably for about half an hour.

The Duke (formerly King Edward VIII) had done his best to

encourage the development of the two training airfields on the island, particularly because of the employment it provided for the local people, most of whom were desperately poor. The Duchess was also very pleasant and I must record that she spent two or three afternoons a week in the Bahamian Club, a servicemen's canteen, where I saw her clearing tables and up to her elbows in the sink washing up. She gave herself no airs, and didn't want to be addressed except as "Madam".

Another lady we met at both the Methodist church and helping in the Bahamian Club was Mrs Brice, a large motherly body who was very friendly. She told us that she had an annexe to her house, a "granny flat" we might call it today. Her sister was staying in it for a while, but when she returned to her own home, we were welcome to stay. We thanked her politely and thought no more about it until we were faced with yet another delay to our training.

A group of ex-operational pilots arrived in the Bahamas to be trained as Liberator captains. Strangely enough one of them was Ken Dart, a contemporary of mine from Christ's Hospital, though as he was a Flight Lieutenant and I was still a Sergeant Pilot, we did not have much opportunity to chat.

As a result our whole course was put on hold for a couple of weeks. We could occupy ourselves in various ways during that time. I spent a week with Air Traffic Control. We could also take a week's leave, but were forbidden to leave the island.

On the very day this news reached us John and I called in at the Bahamian Club and found Mrs Brice on duty. She greeted us by saying, "My sister has now gone back to New York, the annexe is available any time you like to come and stay". So we told her what was happening to us and gladly accepted her offer to spend our week's leave at "Windermere", her home on the coast road just outside Nassau.

The Brice family could not have been more welcoming. They had two cars, one of which they put at our disposal, two boats and a tennis court – a hard one. We saw very little of Mr Brice, an ex-film stunt man who owned a garage, and not much more of the eldest daughter Beverley, aged sixteen, who was away at college most of the time. Two other daughters, twins aged thirteen, Barbara and Brenda, helped their mother entertain us with boat trips and beach picnics. It was idyllic – except that we were constantly aware of the cumulative effect of all these delays on our attempt to join Britain's war effort.

The waiting over, we returned to our course, and were introduced to the Liberator, a big brute compared to anything I had flown before. One hundred and nineteen foot wingspan, and with four Wright Cyclone engines, each consuming thirty-five gallons of fuel per hour at cruising revolutions. We carried out our exercises with our original seven-man Mitchell crew, knowing that under operational conditions this would be increased to ten: two pilots, two navigators, an engineer, wireless operator/mechanic, radar operators and gunners.

My last flight in the Bahamas was a seven-hour operational anti-submarine patrol on 19th July 1943. By then I had flown nearly fifty hours in Liberators and my total flying time was four hundred hours. Now perhaps, we would be allowed to get on with what we had joined up for!

Chapter 5

Introducing 206 Squadron

Leaving the Bahamas, we returned to Miami, thence by train to New York, coming back across the Atlantic aboard the old four-funnel Aquitania to Liverpool. We had no escort just the by now familiar zig-zag course across the ocean. This time the water was considerably calmer and I suffered less. A former single occupancy stateroom had three sets of three decker bunks with room for two sleeping bags on the floor between. Guess who slept on the floor? On the journey my kit and I became separated, the former being discovered back at New York on the return trip. It took several weeks for us to be reunited. In the meantime I was reissued with essentials. Blow me, when the kit bag eventually arrived it had been slit open and the items with which I had been reissued removed. There's efficiency for you.

On 11th August 1943 we arrived at a reception centre in Harrogate. I was now a fully qualified Liberator Captain so was a little surprised to find myself posted within ten days to a squadron flying Fortresses. At the same time my second pilot was posted to North Africa where sadly he was killed within three weeks. On the Fortress I became second pilot to Flight Lieutenant David Beaty a man who had already completed several tours of operations. He took over what had been the rest of my crew. Our training base was Thornaby-on-Tees. There were the makings of two Fortress crews. We learned to fly the Fortress and did some exercises including fighter affiliation near Carlisle with a Beaufighter. The latter could not get his guns to bear as David Beaty could turn the Fortress inside it.

While the Fortress was a beautiful plane to fly, it was not able to carry much weight. The only way we could carry out twelve-hour patrols was by filling the bomb bays with extra fuel tanks, which in turn restricted our offensive armament to only four depth charges, carried under the wings. Unlike the Americans we did not fly the Fortress at any great height and certainly did not carry oxygen. We had more exercises at Thornaby and then from Longtown, followed by bombing practice at Silloth on the Cumbrian Coast. (At the height of the 2001 Foot and Mouth epidemic, RAF Longtown was chosen as the mass burial site for the carcasses of over one million sheep and cattle.)

Exercises completed, we were finally posted to 206 Squadron.

Squadron 206 had a very distinguished history, tracing its origins back to 1st November 1916. In December of that year it left England for Petite Synthe, Dunkirk, France. Originally called No.6 Squadron, Royal Naval Air Service, it operated with Nieuport Scouts and later Sopwith Camels before being disbanded in August 1917.

Within six months it was reformed, flying bombers from Dover on 1st January 1918 and by April of that year, when the RAF came into existence, adopted the designation 206 Squadron RAF. Its greater claim to fame towards the end of World War 1 was as a photography and reconnaissance unit, being so successful that the Army had to request them to stop as they could not cope with the flow of material and information. By this time the squadron was in Germany with the Army of the Rhine operating an Air Mail Service. In June 1918, restored to its bombing role, the squadron moved to Egypt, being redesignated No 47 Squadron on 1st February 1920.

206 Squadron was reformed in 1936 as the RAF prepared for World War Two, becoming the first of several land-based Squadrons of Coastal Command which had hitherto flown Flying Boats. It was equipped with the Avro Anson, a twin-

engined bomber. Early in September 1939 many of the 206 navigators were loaned to Bomber Command for the short-lived bombing sorties against Keil and Brunsbuttel. They were speedily returned being required for important work as convoy escorts, reconnaissance of coastal waters around Holland and Germany, and the increasingly urgent U-boat patrols.

The Squadron's first U-boat contact was made on 5th September when Pilot Officer R T Kean found a U-boat in the act of submerging. Attacking at wave top height, Kean released his bombs, which promptly generated a column of water that split the Anson's tail, though he was able to make it back to base. Four days later the same pilot, clearly attracted to the sea, was forced to ditch in it. Fortunately he was close to the Calais lightship whose crew launched a successful rescue. It rapidly became apparent that the Anson was unsuited for long-range patrol, being replaced by the Lockheed Hudson, an aircraft which soon gained a reputation for giving as good as it got, yet having the capacity to get its crews back to base despite having absorbed heavy punishment.

When in May 1940 the British Expeditionary Force was trapped on the beaches at Dunkirk, 206 Squadron amongst others flew protection patrols over the beaches. On one such on 31st May, Flight Lieutenant "Bill" Biddell in Hudson N7251 engaged nine Messerschmitt Bf109s which were in turn attacking some Fleet Air Arm Blackburn Skuas above him. LAC Walter Caulfield, his air gunner, claimed three enemy aircraft while another Hudson gunner LAC Freeman claimed a further Messerschmitt. Both gunners were later awarded the DFM while Biddell received the DFC. Later the same month Biddell earned another more unusual award for a British pilot. After flying to Bordeaux to evacuate the Polish General Sikorski and his entourage to safety he received the Polish "Cross of Valour" from the General himself.

The redoubtable Pilot Officer Kean found himself in trouble again. While attacking a decoy ship he was jumped by three

Bf109s. His gunner LAC E Townend put paid to one of them before being killed by fire from the two remaining. Kean too had been hit, his co-pilot Sergeant Deverill foiling further attacks by wave skimming tactics, a ploy which was to be used regularly by 206. The remaining Bf109s having fired off all their ammunition eventually wagged their wings in acknowledgement of the Hudson's clever evasion tactics before heading for home. Deverill nursed the Hudson back to base at Bircham Newton where the commanding officer, on examining the two-hundred-and-forty-two bullet holes plus twelve from cannon, declared he had "never seen anything like it".

A squadron crack shot was LAC Deighton who earned a DFM when, after spotting a Bf109 which declined to approach closer, took careful aim at 500 yards' range and shot off its tail!

On 20th March 1941 the Squadron received a new commander, Wing Commander CD Candy RAAF (later, Air Vice Marshall, OBE). Almost immediately his command was decimated when many crew and support staff were posted to form a new Hudson unit, 200 Squadron. They eventually headed for Gambia to perform anti-submarine and convoy duties in the South Atlantic.

Nearer home a Hudson under Pilot Officer Terry Kennan ditched 100 miles west of Ushant after engine failure. The crew successfully evacuated to a dinghy where they were spotted by a Sunderland Flying Boat which, in attempting to land, damaged an engine, thereby thwarting take off. Eventually both crews, by now in dinghies, were rescued by a naval destroyer, after which the Sunderland had sadly to be despatched by gunfire.

In August 1941, to facilitate North Atlantic convoy and U-boat patrol duties, the Squadron moved to Aldergrove, Northern Ireland. During the following winter the Hudsons flew ceaseless patrols in all weathers over the inhospitable ocean. The weather had its plus side, in that U-boats even when sighting a convoy had extreme difficulty in getting a bearing on a potential target. Even when they were on the surface it proved extremely difficult for a trained eye to tell a U-boat wake from the turbulent waters all around. Also on occasion the Hudsons were themselves fired upon by convoy protection vessels, their premise being one of shoot first and identify later.

Nonetheless a year later in February 1942, Group Head-quarters complimented 206 Squadron as, of the six squadrons under its command engaged on similar duties, it had flown 578 out of a total of 1719 hours in the period between 30/12/41 and 2/2/42.

In June of that year twelve Hudsons and crews were detached to North Coates in Lincolnshire under Bomber Command. On the night of the twenty-fifth they took part in the second of Bert Harris's thousand bomber raids on Bremen. Sadly two failed to return, one of which was captained by the Squadron Commander, Wing Commander Cooke, on his first

Fortress FL450 at Benbecula

operational flight with 206. His body and that of his gunner, Flight Sergeant Hubbard were later recovered from the North Sea by the Germans.

By the end of June the Squadron was on the move again, this time to Benbecula in the Outer Hebrides. The following month came news of a change of aircraft, to the four-engined Fortress. The Squadron was taken "out of line" to convert to their new charges which provided far greater range. Initially they were equipped with fourteen depth charges, though this was quickly revised to seven to accommodate a further fuel tank, which extended their range even further to over ten-and-a-half hours. This resulted in a reduction of the yawning gap in the middle of the Atlantic, hitherto out of range from either the UK or Canada, as winter once more approached.

Flying Officer Owen spotted a suspicious object from 8000 feet, straddling it with all seven depth charges. It started emitting oil though of the wrong viscosity as it proved to be a large whale. Over the next three weeks Owen had to stand several rounds at the mess bar, but his keen eyesight was rewarded a few days later when spotting a U-boat a little over a mile ahead. Approaching from astern, six depth charges were dropped as it crash-dived. Photographs taken immediately afterwards showed a large hole torn in the conning tower as the submarine was blown momentarily to the surface before diving again. Owen hung around the area in the hope of finishing it off only to have another U-boat sighted by a crew member. Having only one depth charge left this was dropped from only thirty feet as it dived, again causing the submarine to surface momentarily when a photograph revealed the periscope bent into a loop.

Still Owen's big day was not finished, a third U-boat being sighted two hours later. This time having no depth charges left he made a mock attack forcing a further crash dive. Sadly on his very next mission Owen and all his crew were lost without trace, and this despite three further Fortresses making an exhaustive search of the area.

Early in February 1943 Squadron Leader Patrick, while on routine patrol, was requested by a destroyer towing a corvette to provide air cover. This he did, some two hours later spotting a U-boat which he attacked and sank after it had been bodily lifted out of the water by his depth charges. As a direct result of this action there was introduced into the "Convoy Escort Code" the word "Patrick" meaning, when flashed to a surface vessel: "I am on independent patrol, but can assist you if necessary". Instant fame!

In June, Captain the Right Hon. Harold Balfour, M.C., M.P., commenting on the work of the Command, paid the following tribute:-

Hats off to Coastal Command who, day and night, whatever the weather, fly the Oceans on their allotted duties. Theirs is not the sharp glory of the fighter combat, nor the satisfaction of the con-centrated destruction of Germany's war machine by the bomber offensive. Theirs is a physically arduous and equally hazardous job of flying far out to the West in the front line of the battle of the Atlantic. The tradition of the "Silent Service" must cover the air, and almost complete secrecy enshrouds the activities of the Allied Navies and Air Forces engaged in anti-submarine duties. Give praise to Coastal Command for their unsung glories and feats.

Around this time, the Commanding Officer 206 Squadron was posted to Headquarters, being replaced by Wing Commander R B Thomson, DSO, arriving on the sixteenth of May. Within days he was involved in one of the largest air-sea rescues of the war after taking off from Benbecula in Fortress R/206 on 11th June. At 11.15 hours a submarine sighting was received from R, quickly followed by an SOS, though this faded before a position had been received.

Thomson had in fact sighted a U-boat seven miles ahead and, descending to almost sea level for his run in, was met by an accurate hail of flak, which caused the Fortress to shudder as it absorbed the impact. The Captain dropped his depth charges then turned to circle as the U-boat's bows lifted clear of the water until she was vertical, after which she slid under. Around twenty of her crew were spotted swimming in the water.

At this point number three engine began to pour out smoke followed by the failure of numbers one and two. Petrol and oil were leaking from the wing and height was being lost. The Wing Commander made the decision to ditch while he still had a degree of control. All the crew managed to scramble into the only dinghy which inflated.

Some eight hours later an American Navy Catalina from Iceland circled and attempted a landing. The swell was too great, it hit a big wave, lost its starboard propeller and dived in nose first. The crew clambered out, taking to two life rafts. For some 24 hours both crews could see but not reach each other until, as the weather deteriorated, they drifted apart.

A "fix" had however been established and next day a Fortress flew overhead dropping supplies of fresh water and corned beef which were recovered. Next another Catalina dropped more containers. Later still a Norwegian-crewed Sunderland twice attempted to land only to be bounced back into the air by heavy seas. Another Fortress dropped yet more supplies the following morning plus a message "keep smiling, help coming soon". Two Hampdens from a New Zealand Squadron joined the party by which time the crew of R/206 had so many supplies they had to string them in a line behind the dinghy.

Meanwhile back at Group HQ a hand-picked, and yet all volunteer, crew was about to set forth in another Catalina stripped of all unnecessary gear. Squadron Leader JA Holmes DFC of 190 Squadron took off and reached the rescue scene in some three hours. There was a heart-stopping moment as it made a jarring landing before recovering all eight crew of the Fortress. Tragically, only one of the eight members of the crew of the American Catalina was rescued, by an American destroyer, which threaded its way cautiously through the minefield in which both aircraft had come down.

As a result of Wing Commander Thomson's attack and ditching, partly due to the inadequate forward armament – a Browning .303 machine gun – representations were made for something more substantial. Later Fortresses supplied from America were fitted with a "chin turret" housing twin Browning .5s.

Two months later, the Squadron was "taken out of line" to prepare for movement to an overseas destination, which turned out to be the Azores, which is where we joined them.

Chapter 6

206 Squadron in the Azores

Churchill, in his memoirs, remarked that the one thing that really frightened him was the U-boat menace, and that up to the middle of 1943 we were losing ships faster than they could be replaced. At that point in time he calculated we had eighteen months before being starved into submission.

However in that year the war against the U-boat became more successful, due to several factors. One of these was the use of the airfield in the Azores. From this tiny group of islands, we flew due north to the centre of the Atlantic where the U-boats had formerly been able to strike with impunity, being out of range of both the British and Canadian air cover.

Our base was on the Island of Terceira, from the Portuguese word meaning "third", this being the third island to be colonised from the group of nine inhabited islands. RAF Lagens was built at the site of a grass strip runway, which although both flat and firm enough for dry weather landings, would pose severe problems during the rainy season. Work had begun on a 2000-yard metal strip runway down the middle of a long narrow valley flanked to the west by a 3000-foot mountain.

During the early days there were no "mod cons", the messes were marquees and tents the only billets available. Water had to be laid on, latrines dug and wash-houses provided. Much of the heavy work was carried out by detachments from the Royal Engineers and the R.A.F Regiment.

By the time I arrived, we were billeted in Nissen Huts, situated on a hillside. In the event of being called to duty during the night hours, a low-geared crew transport vehicle would grind its way towards the billets to collect us. There was a rota for call-out duty. The trouble was, you might be fourth or fifth on the list but if there was a "flap" on then any number of crews might have to jump to it. As may be imagined on being woken by the low-geared transport struggling up the hill, the thought which went through everyone's head was, "Are they coming for us or someone else?"

Based alongside us was 220 Squadron, also equipped with Fortresses. Our ranks were further swelled by detachments of Wellingtons, some fitted with Leigh Lights of which more anon, plus Hudsons and a couple of Spitfires.

Our navigators played a vital role; during each long patrol, we flew due north about five hundred miles from the Azores with no artificial navigation aids. The navigators' skill ensured our return to an island ten miles long. Should we miss it there

Lagens Airfield, Azores – General View

Lagens Airfield, Azores – Tented Billets

Lagens Airfield, Azores – Laying the metal strip runway

was nothing else for around a further thousand, the only diversion being to Gibraltar, again a thousand miles distant.
Tragically Flight Sergeant Mitchener and his crew were lost on
28 November 1943 after being diverted, only to find Gibraltar
also closed by fog. My first operational flight was in January
1944, virtually three years since I visited the recruiting office in
1941.

The Portuguese zealously guarded the neutrality of their ter-
ritory, so much so that the RAF were forbidden to fly within
three miles of any of the neighbouring islands. Aircraft returning from patrol were on occasion peppered by over-enthusias-
tic Portuguese anti-aircraft gunners. At Santa Anna, on one of
the other islands in the Azores group, there was a grass airfield,
which, we were told, could be used as an emergency diversion
if the weather closed in at Lagens. I suggested to David Beaty
that if we were to attempt a landing there in bad weather, we
ought first to be allowed to look at it in good weather. David
agreed and obtained the necessary permission, as a result of
which, as a training exercise, two Fortresses flew in from
Lagens ferrying the pilots and navigators from six aircrews.
One Fortress became bogged down in soft ground and, there
being no hope of quick extrication, those deemed most
urgently required back at Lagens returned in the other Fortress;
I was one of those left behind. Our party was conducted under
Portuguese military escort across the intervening hills to the
city of Ponta del Garda. There we dined with the British
Ambassador and slept in the best hotel. A far cry from our
accommodation back at base!

For the rest of the war I served with 206 Squadron on anti-
submarine operations. In the following few paragraphs I paint
in a little background as to what this entailed.

Searching for U-boats involved long weary hours of flying
over the sea, twelve-and-a-half hours being the standard patrol
for our Fortresses. Often we had nothing to show for it, seeing
only sea. Such patrols were however not wasted. The sub-

marines of that time could not travel very far or at any speed under water. So, if the presence of a patrolling aircraft kept them submerged they were largely prevented from getting to where they might do their deadly work.

When a submarine was spotted, we had to act quickly. We carried depth charges, not bombs, and these had to be dropped from only fifty feet above the water, so we never flew very high. Eight-hundred feet was my normal patrol height as in a crash dive a U-boat could be out of range of our depth charges in a matter of seconds. More unpleasantly, instead of diving a U-boat might stay on the surface to fight. This happened more and more towards the end of the war. The 20 and 37 mm cannon fitted on the sub's conning tower could put up a frightening barrage to an aircraft approaching at only fifty feet. Many aircraft were shot down before having the chance to drop their depth charges.

This happened to one of our flight commanders in January 1944 whilst flying out from the Azores. When we were faced with a surfaced U-boat a few weeks later you may well imagine our feelings. It was, I believe, a reporter who witnessed people falling on their knees during the San Francisco earthquake of 1906 who coined the phrase, "there are no atheists in an earthquake". When we arrived safely back from that particular action, the first words of a member of our crew who claimed to be an atheist were, "You were not the only one who was praying, Jim".

This is the story of that action. It was on the night of 12/13 March 1944 that we were called out after Wellington B of 172 Squadron had attacked U-575 on the surface some 500 miles north of the Azores. After the attack the U-boat submerged. Before leaving the area, the Wellington dropped delayed action flame floats. As the next aircraft held in readiness, Fortress R of 206 Squadron was despatched from the Azores to the scene. The Captain was Flight Lt. David Beaty, and at that time I was his second pilot. We took off at 03.27 hours timed to reach the position marked by the Wellington at dawn. Shortly before dawn and having been airborne some three hours, the navigator announced, "We should be about there now, Skipper". As he was speaking I saw from my second pilot's window one of the delayed action flame floats dropped by the departing Wellington. There's navigation for you!

The Wellington had been flying for five hours prior to attacking U-575, and the navigator had determined its position by "dead-reckoning". When flying, it is not only a matter of maintaining the correct course from point A to point B, but also allowance has to be made for wind speed. To achieve this, the navigator is required continuously to make calculations while airborne – a procedure known as dead-reckoning. Over land where there are recognisable features from which to assess the drift this is not too difficult; over water it was necessary frequently to drop smoke or flame floats to permit drift to be measured. This was why I was so impressed by this particular example of dead-reckoning.

David Beaty turned the controls over to me to circle the markers while he crawled forward into the nose to set up a search pattern with our navigator. I continued circling for some twenty minutes as it grew light. When it did so I was amazed to see several large flat patches of water a mile or so across and as still as a millpond. Glass-like.

I had my eyes on one of these patches marvelling at such a sight in the middle of the Atlantic Ocean when, at the very spot I was gazing, U-575 surfaced! I sounded the alarm and commenced a steep diving turn while David scrambled back into his seat. By the time we were low enough to attack, the U-boat had fully surfaced with her 20 and 37 millimetre guns manned.

Having lost the element of surprise, and bearing in mind the recent loss of our flight commander, David decided to try to get a signal to base before attacking. Unfortunately, due to our low altitude, our wireless operator found it impossible to make contact with the Azores, Gibraltar or the UK. We dared not climb

Fortress R/206 at Lagens Airfield, Azores after the attack on U-575

Crew of the Fortress R/206 shown above: Draper, Johnston, Beaty, Glazebrook, MacManus, Meaker and Cunningham

Fl. Lt. Beaty and Fl. Lt. Hart and their crews. Fortress training, Thornaby-on-Tees, September 1943

higher for fear our target would dive. Eventually David enquired of the crew as to whether they were game to have a go without the security of radio contact. We all agreed. David was like that, he was entitled to take the decision himself, but always considered his crew first. As we dived to the attacking height of fifty feet, David corkscrewed on the approach to put off the U-boat's gunners, with our navigator using the nose gun to good effect. The mid-upper turret also fired. Four depth charges were dropped, one on one side of the U boat and three on the other.

After the explosions, the submarine appeared stationary on the surface and then submerged stern first at a steep angle. Oil patches began spreading on the surface. We then climbed, successfully radioing our position, and circled for five hours to guide in Fortress J of 220 Squadron and a naval task group. Shortly after reaching PLE (prudent limit of endurance) we headed back to the Azores. Fortress J arrived, circled the area and noticed an arrowhead to the oilslick showing that the U-boat was moving slowly underwater though still losing oil. J dropped two depth charges, one either side of the arrowhead. More oil surfaced in the form of a roundel. The oil increased considerably though there was no sign of further movement.

Into the area steamed the Canadian frigate, HMCS Prince Rupert, and the United States' destroyers Haverfield and Hobson. They were later able to confirm the sinking of U-575 and the rescue of a number of survivors, including the Captain. The U-boat had been forced to the surface where she was shelled by the ships and attacked further by aircraft from the US escort carrier Brogue.

The kill was officially credited to the three RAF aircraft, aircraft of the United States Navy, two United States' destroyers and the Canadian Frigate. The DFC was awarded to David Beaty.

Chapter 7

Back to Liberators

Less than two weeks after this attack, the Squadron was split up. The older crews nearing the end of their current tour were absorbed into 220 Squadron, while the remainder, eight in number, were ordered to fly back to the UK. We were to leave our Fortresses in England and to travel by train and boat to Northern Ireland for retraining. We didn't know it then but it was less than three months to D-Day and 206 Squadron was scheduled to play an important role in that operation – with Liberators.

We left our Fortresses at Bircham Newton in Norfolk and were rushed in an RAF truck to King's Lynn just in time to catch a train to London. We had an accumulation of baggage, not only our personal belongings, but flying gear, etc – the lot. John and I had between us brought back a large stick of bananas, quite unheard of in England in wartime and this, with some other kit, was left in the corridor. Less than five minutes after leaving King's Lynn I had an uncomfortable feeling and looked out of our compartment just in time to see a soldier taking two bananas off the stick – about twenty had gone already.

Thereupon John and I decided that if others were to have our bananas, we should decide who would receive them. So we walked the length of the train and gave a banana to every child we saw. Most of the little ones didn't know what they were, but their mothers were delighted! John and I still had enough left over to take quite a few home to our families.

Our Liberator conversion course was carried out at

Aldergrove. This gave John Johnston the opportunity to pop home – and indeed to invite all the crew to visit Glenarm, some twelve miles north of Larne, where his parents entertained us to a meal, at which we met two local sisters. Little did I then know that six years later I should return to Glenarm to marry one of them.

It was somewhat frustrating for me having to stand by while David Beaty learned to fly the Liberator; however, there was soon to be a bonus for me. Being already a qualified Liberator Captain, when a few months later a crew became available, I was made up without having to return to the Bahamas for a Captain's course.

By the beginning of June 1944, the invasion of mainland Europe was all set. Crowded onto the single airfield of St. Eval in Cornwall were four Liberator squadrons, thirty or more aircraft. Most of the crews were billeted in the surrounding countryside. Coastal Command's part in the invasion was the aptly named "Operation Cork" with the task of blocking the western end of the English Channel to prevent U-boats from attacking the invasion shipping. This was achieved by setting up three "endless chain" patrols between England and France, so spaced that a U-boat would not be able to cross all three from west to east without surfacing. Each aircraft flew to a strict timetable, so that an observer at any point on each of the three chains would see a Liberator pass every thirty minutes. This was maintained day and night for six weeks. 206 and 547 Squadrons flew through the daylight hours, being relieved at night by 53 and 224 Squadrons, which had been equipped with Leigh Lights for night attacks. On the only two days when fog blanketed St. Eval, the patrols were covered from Northern Ireland.

The Germans, of course, knew of our patrols and made no attempt to run the gauntlet of the Liberators in daylight hours. They did, however, try to break through at night, and one crew of 224 Squadron Captained by Flying Officer Moore, a Canadian, made history by sinking two U-boats in twenty-two minutes. Next morning, the Navy picked up survivors from both.

Unfortunately, there was another hazard to be faced at night. A number of flak ships, no bigger than a surfaced submarine but bristling with anti-aircraft guns, slipped into the Channel at night to decoy the patrolling Liberators. One afternoon shortly after D-Day I met Ken Graves, the lad who had supplied me with apples during that desperate Atlantic crossing in January 1942. He had been flying as a second pilot with 224 Squadron, and said; "This is my last trip tonight before returning to the States for my Captain's course".

It *was* his last trip. That night he was shot down.

A few weeks later, 206 Squadron moved from St. Eval to Leuchars near Dundee in Scotland, and for the rest of the war pursued the enemy in northern waters.

Shortly after our move to Leuchars I was given command of another crew, leaving my original one with David Beaty. Coastal Command had by then adopted the policy that all captains of four-engined aircraft must be commissioned officers. So I was ordered to apply for a commission, and only when I had done so, and passed an interview at Group Headquarters, was my appointment confirmed.

My new crew contained five Australians: we all got on well, but one, Harry Hartwig, my second pilot, was to become a particular friend. Soon winter was approaching and we were reminded that another important factor in our anti-submarine work was the weather. We didn't often see conditions like the day we attacked U-575. The machines we flew in the 1940s were a long way from the all-weather aircraft we boast today. Some conditions over the North Atlantic were quite unflyable, particularly during the winter months. Of the aircraft my Squadron lost during the last year of the war, half were due to atrocious weather. Meteorological forecasting was very limited, there were no satellite pictures then, and out at sea ships and aircraft kept radio silence other than in an emergency. The

My crew at Leuchars, August 1944. Back row: Boorman, Nicholson, Glazebrook, Ellison and Bain; Front Row: Hartwig, Riley, Angel, Smith and McLean

"met" people could tell us very little of what was coming in from the west so when we set off, alone, on patrol, we had little idea of the conditions we might meet. We had to learn to assess them and make our own decisions.

With this background, I hope the reader can appreciate, and to some extent enter into, my feelings as we took off about four o'clock on a wintry morning in one of my first operations as Captain of a Liberator. We were carrying a crew of ten including two pilots. I had spent some months as second pilot but now having a command of my own the responsibility was awesome. Remember this was over sixty years ago and I was "nobbut a lad" as they say in Yorkshire.

The weather was bad as we left our Scottish base and grew progressively worse as we flew westward over the ocean. We reached our allotted patrol area on schedule at dawn and as the darkness turned to a dirty grey the sea below was a terrifying sight. We would not last five minutes if we ditched in that. Frankly I was just plain scared. What was I to do? If we pressed on foolishly in deteriorating weather it might cost us our lives. On the other hand, we had been briefed about a convoy that was due in a few hours. If we turned back, a decision only I could make, and our absence from the area enabled a U-boat to get into position to sink one or more of these ships, the loss of life would be far greater.

So what did I do? The psalmist of old wrote, "In my distress I called upon the Lord and he heard my voice". Well I did just that. I cried from my heart, "Lord what ought I to do?" Most unusually – and this has only happened one other time in my life – I was given an immediate answer. I heard a voice, no, not really a voice though the words came into my head every bit as clearly as if a voice had spoken. I heard words from a psalm written by King David nearly three thousand years ago. Now how in the world can an ancient record like that help my situation? Listen.

"If I take the wings of the morning and remain in the uttermost parts of the sea even there also shall thy hand lead me and thy right hand shall hold me." (Psalm 139)

"The wings of the morning – in the uttermost parts of the sea." It took my breath away. It could not have been more up to date if King David had been a pilot! Anyway, I knew I was being told that we could complete our patrol safely, as we did.

Now, the moral of this story is "Do not believe the fallacy that the Bible is out of date". If it can meet the need of a young inexperienced and frightened pilot over the Atlantic in the 1940s, it can meet anyone's need today. Certainly it is a book written many years ago, or rather a collection of books, yet in a wonderful way it is still the living word of God to man. We neglect its teaching at our peril. True some parts appear obscure and hard to comprehend, but we should not be put off by that. I believe it was the American author Mark Twain who said, "It's not the parts of the Bible I can't understand that worry me, it's the bits I can understand!"

There was one occasion when I did give up through bad weather. We were flying a long rectangle between the Faroes and the Shetlands, this being the route the Germans often sent their U-boats into the Atlantic. It was night. One of the biggest hazards for the Liberator in the winter months was carburettor-icing. The temperature at the manifold is always a few degrees lower than outside. If you were flying just above freezing you got ice building up in the manifold, which reduced your power to the extent that you might end up in the sea.

On my way up from the north of Scotland to the patrol area I had met just such a situation when flying at about 1000 feet. So I came down to something below 500 feet, which cleared the danger. Continuing the long patrol, the weather was deteriorating, and we were tossing around; the wing was going down and coming back up until eventually it went further down, and it took all my strength to fight it. We were almost vertical before making a recovery at which point I thought, enough is enough; I am not risking anything worse than that. Liberators do not fly too well upside down!

I asked the navigator for a course back to Dunnet Head on the north coast of Scotland. Being aware that we should have to go back through the area where the icing problem had occurred, I kept down to 250 feet, easy enough as the Liberator was equipped with a radio altimeter – a sort of set of traffic lights – green indicating the correct height, amber too high, red too low. You simply set the height then watched the lights. I was quite happy flying at this height in the dark over water.

I asked for the ETA (estimated time of arrival) at Dunnet Head to which the navigator responded with a time nearly an hour ahead. Sitting there happily in the dark taking little notice of anything bar the altimeter lights, my reverie was rudely broken by a voice, "Radar operator to Skipper, land is one mile on the starboard beam". I nearly had kittens! We were not due to be near land for at least another forty minutes. Pulling the nose up and pouring on the power I tersely enquired, "How far is it dead ahead?" By pulling the nose up I upset the trim on his radar so it took him ages to give me any answer at all. "For heavens sake tell me something as soon as possible, we are not high enough to clear a blade of grass at present." Something of an exaggeration but it made the point. Then I said, "Navigator, what land was that?" Eventually he came back, "I don't know, Skipper."

In retrospect, we deduced that on the long legs between the Faroes and the Shetlands we had been passing slap through the centre of a depression. The winds had been going right round and the navigator had missed this. The only way he might have assessed it was by dropping flame floats and taking a bearing on them as they passed behind us. He would not always see them in that weather anyway, so missed the wind changes with the cumulative result that we were forty miles east of where he thought we were. We had passed a mile on the wrong side of the island of Foula, which has 1300-foot sheer sea cliffs. We had flown past them at 250 feet. Had we been thirty-seven, thirty-eight or thirty-nine miles out instead of forty this would never have been written.

There was no set pattern to our patrols, simply a pool of Liberator crews available in a set sequence. Each twenty-four hours, Group would call for a certain number of patrols, sometimes two or three, sometimes possibly four or five. A full patrol involved the best part of twenty-four hours. The briefing time before the flight was about three-and-a-half hours preceded by a meal. Then there were pre-flight checks followed by the actual patrol of thirteen-and-a-half hours and finally debriefing and a meal. After any patrol you had a full twenty-four hours before you were back on the roster.

As regards subsistence we were provided with sandwiches and flasks. To fulfil the needs of nature there was a chemical toilet for crew use though the pilots had a pee tube that might be used without leaving your seat. Not to be used when stationary!

One time while I was stationed at Leuchars, I returned from leave on the usual wartime train packed to the gunnels and hours late. Leave officially expired at 23.59 on the date stated on your pass though it was the practice to allow leeway until early the following morning. So that flight crews would not attempt to pinch an extra day, it was invariably arranged that on the morning after your leave had expired, you would be on the schedule for a training flight.

On this occasion I and several of my crew travelled north from London by overnight train. As usual, we were crammed like sardines, squatting on our bags in the corridor. The train was two hours late, so we missed our breakfast and just had time to dump our gear and rush down to sign on for a two-hour training flight at ten o'clock. The rations for such a flight were a two-ounce block of chocolate. So we drew these rations, clambered aboard and commenced our exercise.

U-boats often operated close inshore at this stage of the war so even on training flights we carried full armament. On this occasion we were about halfway through our exercise when a radio message was received telling us to investigate a reported sighting of a periscope off Aberdeen. Off we flew up there and commenced an abortive search pattern for around half an hour. Reporting back to base we were somewhat alarmed to be told, "Remain on patrol until prudent limit of endurance". I enquired of my engineer, "How much fuel have we got Frank?" Back came the reply, "Eight hours Skipper". So, having sat up all night in the train and missed breakfast, we flew nine-and-a-half hours on a two-ounce block of chocolate each!

Thinking about food and moving from famine to feast reminds me of another story concerning the crew of a Short Sunderland. This was recounted by Chaz Bowyer in his book "Men of Coastal Command 1939–1945" (William Kimber 1985). These aircraft, in their guise as the Empire Flying Boats, were the bees-knees of domestic flights prior to WWII. Now, adapted for use by Coastal Command they performed similar duties to ourselves.

Amongst the facilities available on board was a well-equipped galley. So commodious was this aircraft in general terms that some crews preferred to live on board rather than in some of the rather spartan camps that had sprung up in response to wartime requirements. On this particular aircraft, one of the gunners doubled up as cook. He had by some doubt-less questionable tactics contrived to obtain not only a huge two-inch thick steak but also a selection of vegetables. When you remember that the more usual fare was spam or spam, it is not difficult to envisage the anticipation with which this repast was viewed. The gunner/cook tantalised the crew with peri-odic countdowns as to when lunch would be served, only to be thwarted at the eleventh hour by the sighting of a U-boat and the resultant call to action stations. The Sunderland dived to and successfully straddled the submarine with its depth charges though absorbing some punishment in return from a deck-mounted cannon.

Resuming its more sedate cruising pattern the Captain enquired after delayed lunch whereupon the gunner reverted to his secondary role disappearing once again into the galley. For some long time there was neither sight nor sound of him until, seemingly hours later, he emerged triumphant to serve steak and vegetables to the grateful crew. When they had fin-ished, someone remarked on the unusual flavour of the meat whereupon the cook felt bound to confess that the steak had been lost during the attack, and that he had had considerable difficulty in relocating it. Eventually he had found it in the bilge from where it had been recovered with a length of bent wire more generally used for clearing the sink waste pipe. He had however thoroughly washed the recovered item with cold tea before giving it a really good grilling.

The remainder of this particular flight was completed in silence.

Chapter 8

The Last Months of WWII in Europe

When we watch a passenger jet take off today, we see it getting airborne halfway along the runway, pointing its nose skyward then soaring upward at a phenomenal rate. That says much about the fantastic power of modern jet engines. It is also evidence of the international civil aviation regulations that quite rightly insist on large margins of safety for passenger flying operations.

It wasn't like that during the war – there was just no safety margin. A fully laden Liberator, with all four engines at maximum power, and with no wind to assist, often lifted off with only 100 yards of a standard 2000-yard runway remaining, followed by a very shallow climb.

Early one morning during July 1944, one of our squadron pilots, F/L John Hancock, was setting off with his crew on an anti-submarine patrol when something caused him to abandon take off. But he was going too fast to pull up, and ran off the end of the runway and then some distance over the rough ground beyond before coming to a stop. A few seconds later 2000 gallons of petrol and twelve 250lb depth charges went off in a colossal explosion that shook the whole station.

I had been asleep at the time, and woke suddenly, conscious of some abnormality but heard nothing for about thirty seconds until the explosion took place. We were used to having aircraft taking off at all hours of the day and night and a normal take off would not have disturbed me. Somehow, as soon as that pilot cut his throttles in an attempt to stop, my sub-conscious recognised that something was wrong and I woke immediately.

The explosion killed both pilots and six other crew members. Miraculously, and there is no other word to describe it, the navigator and a gunner escaped with a few scratches, and after a couple of days in the station sickbay returned to duty.

Not long after, the navigator, a big burly Canadian, came out of his room near to mine using a stream of the foulest language imaginable. I didn't know what it was all about though I felt I ought to say something like, "didn't your experience the other morning teach you anything – you ought to be thanking God for saving your life instead of blaspheming his name in that way?" I ought to have said that but I didn't. I just curled up inside and held my tongue.

Just two months later, I and my crew spent all one night on patrol off Norway. For nine hours in darkness, we flew a long narrow rectangular course parallel to the coast. Seven times we completed this circuit and, each time approaching the southern end on the leg nearest the mainland, we passed within sight of Sola, which was, and still is, the airfield for Stavanger. At that time it was a German fighter station. Twice they put up aircraft to intercept us, but we evaded them by getting really low over the water. I knew the fighters wouldn't risk firing at us so close to the surface at night. A combination of being dazzled by the flashes from their own guns and a momentary loss of control from the recoil of their cannon meant a real risk of their hitting the sea. So on both occasions they shadowed us from above for a while then turned away.

At the end of our time in the area, we set course for base while our place on the rectangular patrol was taken by another crew from the squadron, piloted by F/O Carlisle. Daylight came by the time we were halfway home and with it our wireless operator picked up an SOS from the other aircraft. The fighters that dared not fire at us in the dark came out and attacked our relief in daylight and shot him into the sea.

206 Squadron Liberator over Trevose Head, June 1944. This aircraft (EV885) was shot down after relieving me off the coast of Norway on 28 September 1944.

There were no survivors.

The crew that perished included both men who had escaped the take-off crash in July. So that Canadian navigator was granted just two months of extra life, two months in which to repent of his Godless attitude, and I, the only Christian, as far as I know, who was given the opportunity of warning him, failed to take it.

Liberators were strong and resilient. On the 15th November 1944, Flying Officer Frost and his crew were on patrol off the Norwegian Coast when they were attacked by three Messerschmitt 110 twin-engined fighters. The enemy attacked on no less than nine occasions, coming in very fast just above sea level so that although the radar operator picked them up over eight miles away, they were but 400 yards off when spotted with the naked eye.

In the first attack an engine was knocked out, the constant speed unit being completely shot away, so that the propeller could not be feathered. This "windmilling" engine reduced the speed from 190 to 150 knots and also cut down the range of evasive options. Next the hydraulic system was disabled, meaning that the depth charges could not be jettisoned. During one of the early attacks the port beam gun was hit and the gunner, Sergeant Conway, was killed. More was to follow.

Next to go was the intercom, forcing the second pilot to relay messages from the mid-upper turret to the Captain, who then took such evasive action as he was able. The wireless operator had already sent an enemy aircraft signal. Now he changed to medium frequency and sent an SOS, though as his receiver had been hit he had no way of knowing whether or not his messages had been received. Then the rear turret was hit, putting one gun out of action and wounding the gunner, Flight Sergeant Nicholson, in the leg. He continued firing with the remaining gun until that seized up, after which he crawled from the turret and applied a tourniquet to his shattered leg. Now the fighters concentrated on attacking astern until the mid upper gunner Flight Sergeant Gollan, hit and set on fire the port engine of one of them, at which they all turned tail.

A check on the damage by the engineer revealed, in addition to that already mentioned, there were many holes in the wings and fuselage; one aileron half-shot away, plus the greater part of one of the elevator control surfaces and a large section of rudder. The engineer finally prised apart the bomb doors through which thankfully the depth charges were jettisoned. A crash landing was eventually made at Sumburgh in the Shetlands. Flying Officer Frost later received the DFC for this action while DFMs were awarded to Gollan and Nicholson, the latter's shattered leg having to be amputated.

During these winter months, though operations continued, they were on a reduced scale in order to permit the Squadron to be equipped with Leigh Lights. The Leigh Light, so named after its inventor, Wing Commander Leigh, generated some 20 million candlepower, and was designed to illuminate a target one mile ahead. The huge light was suspended under the starboard wing and weighed in the order of one ton.

The apparently simple addition of a searchlight for night attacks involved more headaches than would at first seem possible. A phenomenal amount of intensive and arduous training was necessary to acquire the correct co-ordination between pilot, radar operator and the Leigh Light operator cum bomb aimer. Night after night the training sorties continued, making practice runs forwards and backwards across Bell Rock lighthouse, the "Mark V" training buoy and any conveniently placed shipping in the area. Later exercises were arranged with an Allied submarine stationed at Dundee. Occasionally aircrew

The Leigh Light installed under a Liberator's starboard wing

went out in the submarine, and members of the submarine's crew were carried in the exercising aircraft. Neither was attracted to the other's environment!

One aircraft was lost in the course of this training. On the night of 2nd December 1944, Q/206 caught fire and plunged into the sea off Crail. The pilot was Squadron Leader RH Harper, DFC, who won his decoration as a flying officer with 206 Squadron in 1940; the crew contained a number of 206 veterans from the Azorean days. Search was made throughout the night and the following day, but the cold grey sea revealed no trace of those she had claimed; the only sign of the wrecked aircraft appeared some days later, when one of Q's wheels was washed up onto the stormy shore near St. Andrews.

In early February 1945 Coastal Command decided on a mass attack – an all-out offensive, under the code name Operation Chilli, against the U-boat training grounds in the Baltic Sea. Fourteen Liberators, all equipped with Leigh Lights, were to take part, seven each from 206 and 547 squadrons.

We left RAF Leuchars in a blinding snowstorm and on the journey eastward lost two of our number. D/206, piloted by Squadron Leader Graham, had an engine fire on take-off, and jettisoned his depth charges and Leigh Light immediately. The latter scored a direct hit on a house in Dundee, fortunately without casualties. The weather was too bad for Squadron Leader Graham to land at Leuchars and he had to be diverted to Wick.

B/206 captained by Flight Lieutenant Haggas was shadowed, then attacked by three enemy aircraft whose attentions were repeatedly foiled by skilful evasive action directed by the radar operator. However so much fuel was used, that Flight Lieutenant Haggas had to turn back before reaching the Baltic.

With the Germans occupying Denmark and Norway, we knew we were running the gauntlet of the enemy on both sides of us. For this reason, the entire operation was carried out at or below 200 feet. Flying just above the sea north-east up the

Skagerrak, we then turned almost due south around the north-ernmost tip of Denmark and down the Kattegat between Denmark and Sweden. Finally we swung east around the foot of Sweden into the Baltic.

By employing these tactics we avoided radar detection and achieved complete surprise. I first dropped six depth charges on a 2000-ton coaster, and, just as I did so my radar operator found a further contact some ten miles away. This turned out to be a flotilla of five U-boats plus destroyer escort.

The navigator got on to the Leigh Light from where he effectively became the bomb aimer. When he heard from the radar operator that the target was one mile away, he switched on the Light. The best laid plans of mice and men … !!

Unfortunately, and this did not become apparent until next day, each time the front gunner moved his hydraulically-operated turret to the left it put a short circuit on the intercom. So, in this turret position when the radar operator called "one mile", nobody heard him. By the time the gunner had swept his turret to the right, the "three-quarters-of-a-mile" was heard, and the Leigh Light belatedly switched on, and so shone beyond the target, not on it, with the result that the navigator never saw it, though most of the rest of the crew did.

There were five stationary U-boats, all carrying riding lights, plus a destroyer. The amazing fact was, the whole lot were seemingly fast asleep – but not for long. The navigator not having seen the target no depth charges were released, we simply flew at mast height right over them.

I thought to myself "that's torn it, they might have been asleep a couple of minutes ago – they won't be when I come back". I had the alternative of forgetting about the attack, and flying back home to await court martial for not doing the job for which I had been trained, or I could turn around and fly into the jaws of death, a Liberator being no match for a Narvik class destroyer.

I reasoned to myself that assuming they had raised the

alarm, the U-boats should by now be getting under way. They had to be moving to submerge and this would leave a wake. Now there was supposed to have been a moon that night but cloud obscured it. However it was not pitch black so I said we would go back, but requested the navigator not to use the Leigh Light if he could see anything at all.

We returned. Sure enough the U-boats were all under way, and our navigator bombed on the wakes. Now there was another instance of what I consider to be Divine intervention. In a large aircraft the first pilot sits on the left and, if you want to make a violent manoeuvre you would normally turn left, as it is far easier to see through your side window what you are doing. The instant the navigator said, "Bombs gone", the term being used with impunity also for depth charges, I threw the Liberator over to the right without thinking. As I did so, the destroyer opened up and all the flak came up past my left wingtip missing us completely. Had I gone the other way we should have been hit in a big way. We headed for home via Sweden where we were shot at again but not hit.

Remember my old friend and pilot David Beaty from my first encounter with a U-boat? Well he, too, had homed onto the same target as I, though a few minutes later. So, when he commenced his bombing run and switched on his Leigh Light one mile out, his aircraft caught all the flak from the destroyer intended for me! One of his engines was shot out and two others damaged; the mainplanes and rudders were extensively damaged. The bomb bay doors would not close and a gun position had a hole blown in it. The engineer, after assessing the damage, announced laconically, "We've had it, Skipper". However, David managed to gain some height and decided that as he was unable to take any evasive action if attacked by a fighter, he would make for Sweden and the crew and he would bail out.

Now, apart from the pilots, who sit on their parachutes, the rest of the crew wear parachute harness, the parachute pack being a separate item that clips on, if and when needed. Coastal Command never thought about bailing out, as we flew far too low anyway. In the darkness and subsequent panic, one chap picked up his parachute, not by its handle but by the ripcord. The parachute opened inside the aircraft adding further to the general melee. The owner of this item announced his intention of bundling the parachute under his arm and jumping out with it. David would have none of it, as he thought it likely that it would wrap itself around the tail and go down with the plane.

As he still had some sort of control of the Liberator, David decided they would take a chance, and try to make it home, which they eventually did making a crash landing at Banff. The aircraft was so badly damaged that it took the combined strength of both pilots to hold a straight course. Subsequent examination by the ground crew found over 600 holes, yet not one member of the crew was injured – physically.

Two weeks later Flight Lieutenant Beaty received a bar to his DFC earned in our previous joint encounter and I received a DFC. David could have had one or two choice comments to make to me regarding meeting all that flak generated by our two earlier bombing runs, though he never referred to it. We were to remain firm friends until his death in December 1999. After the war he became a civilian pilot and also a very fine writer with a string of books to his name. His biography, written by his wife Betty Campbell Beaty, is entitled *"Winged Life"* and was published by Airlife Publishing in July 2001.

Towards the end of the war, Sid Banks, a navigator on the squadron, declined to go on a period of leave. Instead he chose to fly with Bomber Command just as it were for the hell of it. On one of the daylight heavy bomber raids over Germany he was standing literally as spare man behind the pilot of a Lancaster as they ran over the target. He happened to glance up, and there directly above them was a Halifax just opening its bomb doors!

Sid swiftly drew this unfortunate turn of events to the attention of the pilot, who immediately kicked hard on right rudder and slid out of the line of fire as the bombs whistled past them. When the pilot had recovered his composure, Sid enquired: "What would have happened if this had been a night operation?" "Simple, we should not have seen them!" was the reply. There were many accidents caused through incidents of that ilk – collisions or being struck by our own bombs.

In April 1945, for operational reasons, we were asked to go on leave earlier than originally scheduled. This presented a problem for George Ellison, one of my gunners who had planned to get married on the day our leave had been due to start. He came to me in an understandably distressed condition. I went to the Gunnery Officer with George's predicament; he likewise sympathised, and arranged that George should assist him in the office, while my crew were on our leave. When George was on his honeymoon, we would be provided with a spare gunner.

Whilst we were on leave, another crew was short of a gunner. George stepped quite literally into the breech. He and all this crew were lost on an operation in the Kattegat. George's was the only body washed up onto the coast, where it was recovered and given a full military funeral by the Swedish authorities.

On 3rd May 1945, Liberators C/206 with Flight Lieutenant Beaty in command, and E/206 captained by myself were once again in the Kattegat on anti U-boat patrol. Reaching the eastern end of the Skaggerak we found the entire area between the Danish and Swedish coasts to be a mass of shipping. All carried riding lights; all were steaming north in orderly rows. We were witnessing the mass Nazi evacuation from Denmark to Norway, though it was not without its moments of apprehension, shadowed as we were by German fighters though they never attempted to attack us. The following morning the remaining German forces in Denmark and North Germany surrendered. We had witnessed a small part of history being created.

Liberator L/206 off the Scottish Coast, March 1945

That same day another Liberator sighted and attacked U-534 in the Kattegat. The signs were that this attack was successful; after the war it emerged that U-534 had sailed from Keil carrying a contingent of high-ranking Nazis who were fleeing justice. There was even a suggestion that Martin Bormann might have been amongst their number. In fact U-534 had been sunk and was raised during 1993 from its resting place off Anholt Island by a Danish salvage team. There were fifty-three people on board at the time of its sinking, far more than a normal crew. The majority were picked up by German E-boats.

Those surviving members of the crew of U-534, on being interviewed after the war, said that the nature of their mission had never been revealed to them. The class of U-boat was in itself of significance – Type 9-C having a range of 11, 400 miles. On board U-534 was an Argentinean radio operator, plus supplies sufficient to reach South America. These included several

Surrendering U-boat, U-1231, North of Butt of Lewis, 13th May, 1945

cases of vintage 1936 wine. U-534's wreck was discovered, and then recovered by Danish divers, and from 1996 has been berthed at Birkenhead. After the German capitulation, 206 Squadron continued its patrols around the Kattegat, returning crews witnessing scenes of jubilation while crossing Denmark. Sweets and chocolates were dropped by our crews flying low over the streets below. The last of these was captained by Flight Lieutenant Pearce flying from Leuchars on 7th May, being the last fully operational sortie before VE-Day.

When the war in Europe ended, over 200 U-boats were still at sea. They were ordered by radio to sail on the surface and fly a black flag of surrender, and then proceed to various ports in Scotland. Coastal Command continued their anti U-boat patrols to escort these vessels in. We were told clearly the instructions given to the U-boat captains, and if these were not obeyed, for example by submerging or proceeding at periscope depth, we were to attack notwithstanding the war being over.

One day I found a U-boat trying to sneak past the north of Scotland at periscope depth, obviously hoping to get back to Germany rather than be escorted into a Scottish port. In accordance with my instructions, I prepared to attack, opened the bomb bay and commenced an attacking run. He must have been keeping an eye on me through his periscope, for he came very rapidly to the surface and put out his black flag of surrender. As we flew down low beside him the officers stood in the conning tower and gave a Nazi salute. One of my gunners wanted to give them a quick burst, but I drew the line at that! We radioed his position, and then escorted him until relieved by another aircraft.

"Jack" Frost, the pilot who had fought that running battle with the Me110s off Norway was at this time flying over the North Sea when he found a U-boat heading for Denmark. He signalled it to stop, which the boat did and then to turn round and proceed in the opposite direction. The Captain pretended not to understand, continuing once more towards Denmark. At this Jack dropped a depth charge in front of the bow of the U-boat; this assisted the Captain's comprehension no end and he came swiftly into Dundee. With a few others from our base at RAF Leuchars, I went to Dundee and boarded the U-boat, a miniature one with a crew of barely ten or eleven. I spoke with the Captain, each having a smattering of the other's language. He boasted that his U-boat could stay submerged for up to eighty-one days. I could think of little worse than being cooped up in a tin box under the sea for that length of time. I put it to him that this must be a great strain, to which he retorted, "No, the longer we can stay submerged, the less likely we are to be attacked by aircraft". So that was their big fear towards the end of the war.

Chapter 9

Conversion to Transport Command

After the war in Europe had ended, we changed our role. Our Liberators were altered to become troop carriers, flying between the UK and India to supply the Far Eastern theatre, it being envisaged that the war with the Japanese might go on for some time.

The gun turrets were removed and the doors sealed on the bomb bays, which were then transformed into compartments for eighteen troops, nine each side, facing each other, knees almost touching and doubtless very uncomfortable. A further eight travelled in the tail section in considerably more comfort. In addition there was a crew of five. The Liberator was about the largest plane available at the time though later the York, based on the Lancaster, fulfilled a similar role.

At this time, Transport Command took over a number of Coastal Command Squadrons and sent a team of their senior officers from station to station to instruct the aircrews involved. The commanding officer of each station visited was charged with the responsibility of providing transport for the team to the next port of call. On 13th June 1945 I was detailed to fly the Transport Command team from Leuchars to Ballykelly in Northern Ireland. (A unique feature of Ballykelly was that the Belfast to Londonderry railway line crossed the main runway. Close communication was crucial between Flying Control on the airfield and the railway signal box to ensure there was no conflict between trains and aircraft!) My passengers included a Group Captain, a Wing Commander and three Flight

Lieutenants from Transport Command, along with five others (ex-547 Squadron) and three members of my crew.

The Group Captain at Leuchars gave me a brief lecture before the flight, emphasizing the importance of delivering my VIPs safely to Ballykelly. Then, obviously conscious that his responsibility was not discharged until they had arrived, he called into the Leuchars Flying Control about an hour-and-a-half after I took off, enquiring of the duty controller: "Is there any news of Glazebrook's arrival at Ballykelly yet?" "No sir, but he should be getting there about now." At that very moment, my voice was heard on the VHF receiver at Leuchars calling Ballykelly Flying Control for landing instructions. To have been heard at Leuchars when I was overhead at Ballykelly 250 miles away was quite a freak, as the voice frequency radios of those days normally had a range of about ten miles, and were only used by an aircraft in the vicinity of its base.

For the India run our home base was at Oakington just outside Cambridge. (These days it is an Army base, finding recent use as a temporary home for asylum seekers.) I made two return training runs to India before going operational.

The first operation was combined with a further necessity. At that time there was concern about a possible uprising in Palestine, and it was decided to move a number of troops from Europe to the Middle East. We were to pick them up at Melsbroek, a military airfield outside Brussels, taking them via North Africa to Cairo; each of three squadrons would fly out one aircraft every twenty-four hours. On 12th October 1945 we were to fly out to Belgium empty, collecting twenty-five passengers plus a Wing Commander Barker before proceeding to Castel Benito near Tripoli, a journey of some seven or eight hours. The crew who had gone out twenty-four hours previously would take over after the plane had been refuelled and the passengers fed, and then fly on to Cairo.

This then is the background to one of my most terrifying experiences.

Now you may recall that a fully-laden Liberator needed the best part of 2000 yards to get airborne. We arrived and landed at Melsbroek on what turned out to be a 1850-yard runway. There was no wind to assist and we were expected to take off with troops who had come straight from action in North West Europe laden down with war souvenirs of all descriptions in addition to all their kit. Nobody made any attempt to weigh them. To balance the weight distribution of the aircraft, the Navigator was surrounded by kit bags.

I had no means of judging how heavy we were, though clearly well over the safety margin. Frankly I was scared that we should not get off this runway, so after speaking to the other two pilots on the same schedule, we went along to flying control where we tried unsuccessfully to make our point. An additional complication was that our schedule provided for a night-time departure. The technique for taking off a heavily-laden Liberator involved lifting the nose wheel as soon as possible, and then lifting up the nose slightly, but not too much, until flying speed was reached. It was harder to judge the right attitude for this in the dark. We asked if we might leave an hour earlier, in daylight, but to no avail.

We were fed the usual flannel: "The schedule has been fixed by Group. We cannot alter it. Liberators have been taking off from this runway all week. You're good pilots, otherwise you wouldn't have been given this job." And so on. At this the other two pilots gave in. I was still not happy though a little later, talking to my engineer, I learned something which perhaps in retrospect I should have known. The aircraft power is measured by the pressure at the point where the fuel enters the engine manifold, the normal take-off figure being forty-eight inches of mercury. Once airborne you would throttle back to thirty-five inches for the climb to operating height.

Frank Angel, my engineer, told me that he could adjust the engines to deliver emergency power of fifty-two inches, which is what we decided to do. This would put the engines under some considerable strain, so I should throttle back as soon as possible once airborne. Fully laden we trundled round the taxi way until I was able through careful positioning to place the Liberator right on the end of the runway, the wheels balanced just on the tarmac. Had they run off I feel sure we should have sunk right into the mud.

Holding her on the brakes I revved up the engines until the engineer gave me the thumbs up that we had maximum power. Releasing the brakes, we moved off down the runway, accelerating all too slowly. As the red light at the end of the runway approached our speed reached around ninety-five mph, too slow I feared with this load to become safely airborne. When the red light disappeared under the nose of the plane, I desperately pulled back on the control column, not actually the best method of getting off. We did lift, then bounced, and I swear to this day that was on the perimeter track. Fortunately there were no trees ahead and I kept on maximum power for a few more seconds before throttling back to forty-eight inches. It still took a full ten minutes to achieve 1000 feet. Not a happy situation.

We flew through the night of 12th/13th October to Castel Benito. The following day I waited for the next 206 Squadron aircraft to arrive which I should take on to India. It never made it, having crashed on take-off. All thirty-one on board were killed. Later I heard that after that they cut down the maximum load for take off by 5000 pounds. I made three round trips to India, during the third of which I had a total of twenty-four hours' sleep in six days. Feeling quite shattered and sporting a hacking cough, which refused to go away, I visited the Medical Officer who promptly grounded me for six months.

The Squadron C.O. was faced with finding something useful for me to do during this period and suggested I might write the history of 206 Squadron. This certainly appealed to me and I promptly accepted with the proviso that I tackle it my own way. "Show me what you have in mind", was his response, so

I wrote a couple of chapters that appeared to meet with his approval. To collect the necessary data, I went to search the records at Coastal Command Headquarters, Northwood.

At lunchtime on my first day, feeling rather nervous, I joined the queue at the officers' mess. In peacetime officers are waited on, but in a war situation on an RAF station only the top table comprising the Group Captain and two Wing Commanders are served, everyone else having to queue for their meals at the hatch. Glancing back, I was staggered to see an Air Vice Marshal immediately behind me in the queue; the only people waited on here were the Air Officer Commanding and the C in C.

By the end of the six months, I had completed my "War History of 206 Squadron", a precis of which I have already included in these pages. I added seven appendices listing Commanding Officers of the Squadron, Locations, Aircraft, Duties, U-boat "kills" (of which there were twelve), Roll of Honour (274 casualties) and Decorations and Awards (94).

As a prologue I quoted verses from Ecclesiasticus, a chapter that was regularly read in the leaving service at the end of each term at Christ's Hospital.

1. Let us now praise famous men, and our fathers that begat us.
2. The Lord hath wrought great glory by them through his great power from the beginning …
8. There be of them, that have left a name behind them, that their praises might be reported.
9. And some there be, which have no memorial.
10. But these were merciful men, whose righteousness hath not been forgotten
15. The people will tell of their wisdom, and the congregation will show forth their praise.

Ecclesiasticus, 44

Unfortunately by the time the history was finished at the end of April 1946, the Squadron was once more temporarily disbanded. With no photocopying machine in those days, the best we could do was to use the station duplicator to run off 150 copies, which we sent to those members and ex-members of the Squadron whose addresses were known.

I was transferred to Station Headquarters, Oakington, where I became P.A. to the Station Commander, Group Captain Chisholm. As a regular officer, he was allowed a month's End of War leave, and being from Southern Ireland he determined to fly up to Valley (Anglesey) from where he could get a boat to Dublin. He had the use of an Oxford twin-engined communications machine, and he said to me: "Find me an Oxford pilot to come with me to RAF Valley, then I can get a boat from Holyhead to Ireland and he can fly the plane back." Off I went round the station trying to find a volunteer, though with a conspicuous lack of success. It was the VJ weekend, and most officers were going on leave.

In desperation I had to confess no qualified Oxford pilot was available, though offering to fly the plane myself as I had on occasion unofficially flown an Oxford. Really he should have checked me out but this went by the board. At the appointed hour we met up with a couple of chaps who wanted dropping off at RAF Sealand, near Chester, on the return leg. The Oxford in question did not even boast dual controls. The Group Captain ordered me to fly it, so I flew up to Valley with him sitting beside me and made the most appalling landing.

The Oxford was difficult to land well; anyone who flew one said so. We bounced down that runway like a kangaroo before turning off and coming to a shuddering halt. There was a long silence before: "I suppose if I don't sign your log book you can't go home?"

"No Sir", handing it over.

He signed it: "Qualified to fly an Oxford. 7th June 1946"!

He got out, doubtless thankfully, and I flew the other two –

who had remained silent throughout – to RAF Sealand. After that I flew solo back to Oakington where I made a much better landing by myself.

Chapter 10

The Origins and Development of MAF

While still at Oakington, we had a visit from a New Zealand pilot Trevor Strong, who had been stationed there more than a year earlier when it was a bomber station, home to Number Seven Squadron flying Lancasters. One night they were sent to attack a target in Northern Italy. On his way home across France, Trevor was attacked by an enemy aircraft, which set both starboard engines on fire.

After unsuccessfully trying to douse the flames Trevor decided that he must abandon the aircraft, holding it level as one by one the other six members of his crew dived out of the hatch. Then he knew it was his turn to go, though he felt a strange or then again not so strange reluctance to jump, never having used a parachute before. He had, of course, been taught how to use one, and had talked to others whose lives had been saved by them; but to put his trust in that previously untried means of escape by leaping into the dark was quite a different matter. On the other hand, sitting in the pilot's seat he was doing something with which he was familiar, having at least some control of the aircraft.

He knew in his heart that he could not delay indefinitely. The fire was spreading and, when it reached the main fuel tanks it was more than likely that the wing would blow off, and the Lancaster go down in an uncontrollable spin, giving him little chance of escaping.

Eventually he overcame his reluctance and jumped, spending the remainder of the war in a POW camp. At Oakington and again to 8000 young people in the Royal Albert Hall, London, I heard him use his story to illustrate the process of becoming a Christian. Just as he had been sitting in the pilot's seat, we control our lives by doing what we're used to. We are reluctant to let go of ourselves and make that leap of faith using the parachute that Jesus has provided for us by his death on the cross. We should trust in him to save us and guide us to a secure landing. Others may have proved that it works, and seek to reassure us – but the actual first step of committing our lives to Christ is something that noone else can do for us – we've got to jump for ourselves.

That pilot's visit to Oakington was not just a nostalgic return

Keith Jones, Chief Executive of MAF/UK

The Maasai are a nomadic people hard to evangelise; much has been achieved by Pastor Lemashon, a Masai with a passion for reaching his own people. Some of his flights with MAF have been sponsored by UK supporters. This Maasai mother and her baby are seen beneath the wing of MAF Cessna at Malam.

to the base from which he had taken off on that fateful operation. During his time in the POW camp he had thought, talked and prayed with like-minded others of putting the aviation skills learned in war to aid medical, missionary and relief work. In many parts of the world surface travel is time-consuming, and often difficult; in some seasons and places it is quite impossible. The vision he shared with us, and with other Christian groups in the RAF, gave rise to the organisation we now call Mission Aviation Fellowship.

Accompanying Trevor Strong on that nostalgic return to Oakington was another New Zealand pilot, Murray Kendon, who had flown with Coastal Command throughout the war years. Stuart King, in his book "Hope has Wings", was to write of Murray:

The arrival of the plane is always greeted with enthusiasm, especially by the children.

Long hours of patrol over the grey waters of the Atlantic had given him plenty of time to ponder. He thought about the power and versatility of aircraft, of all the Coastal Command planes on patrol, of bomber, transport, fighter and ground attack aircraft. Command of the skies had been decisive in the Battle of Britain, the Mediterranean, North Africa, Asia and the invasion of Europe. Man had learned to fly; was such knowledge and experience to be devoted only to conflict?

From childhood, Murray had had the privilege and influence of a Christian family. He'd felt a particular concern for the millions of people who lived, impoverished and fear-ridden in isolated places – mountains, deserts, jungles or swamps. He was convinced that more should be done to reach them. He believed that planes could be used to bring them help and hope. To show them God's love. To do so in partnership with overseas churches and missions.

But how might it be done? Murray felt strongly that aviation

Christian Blind Mission is one of the organisations regularly using MAF to carry teams to operate in remote places.

A Cessna Caravan aircraft in Madagascar; this large island is one of the most difficult areas for surface travel.

should not be taken as a sideline by missions, even where it was greatly needed. Such an approach would be neither efficient nor safe.

In fact, there had been certain pioneering efforts. The Reverend Harold Shepherdson, a Methodist missionary in Northern Australia, had recognised the need for an aircraft in the Arnhem Land work as early as 1931, and Keith Langford-Smith of the Church Missionary Society had operated a Gipsy Moth in missionary work in the early 1930s.

Then there was George Fisk, who flew a biplane "stagger wing" Beechcraft in Borneo, and Paul Carlson of the Evangelical Mission Church who took a Fairchild 24 to Alaska for his work. World War Two later interrupted the work of both Fisk and Carlson. Fisk's Beechcraft had to be destroyed to keep it out of the hands of the invading Japanese, while wartime storage regulations forced Carlson to sell his Fairchild.

Wally Herron returned to Bolivia with a Piper P5 and established a permanent service in the area he covered, flying regularly until he was killed in a Cessna he had just purchased to extend the work. His son Robert continues to this day. (After telling this story at a meeting I took in the Lake District a few years ago, a missionary in the audience came to me afterwards and said, "Yes, you are right, Robert is still flying in Bolivia; I was at his wedding there last year".)

Nevertheless, Murray Kendon was right in saying missionary flying was a task for specialists. This was being increasingly recognised by a number of World War Two airmen who had the same vision of using their skills in the service of God. Across the Atlantic, the Christian Airmen's Missionary Fellowship numbered among its members Charles Mellis, Grady Parrott, Betty Greene and Jim Truxton, names that were to become synonymous in post-war years with the development of missionary aviation throughout the world. (I met Jim Truxton at US/MAF Headquarters in Redlands, California in 1982. He trained as I did at Pensacola.) Subsequently, as a result of a conference between

Harry Hartwig at my aunt's home, "Barn Mead", Ingatestone

the British and American groups in 1947, the Americans also decided to adopt the name Missionary Aviation Fellowship.

The work of the Australian MAF began through the vision of Harry Hartwig, my second pilot in 206 Squadron from August to December 1944. While involved on the Squadron he solemnly covenanted with God that, if he survived, he would seek to bring aeroplanes and pilots back to New Guinea to carry the message of peace for all mankind.

In preparation for possible missionary service, Harry enrolled in a two-year course at the Melbourne Bible Institute. His application to the Australian Government for a grant was turned down. The authorities made it a condition that grants would only be given to ex-service personnel whose service in the forces had demanded exceptional ability. Harry believed that what been required of Coastal Command Captains, flying on lone operations without the company of other fighters or bombers, met this condition. So he wrote to ask for my help; from a former Flight Commander on the Squadron, by that time serving in the Air Ministry, I obtained both a description of the qualities needed in a Coastal Command Captain, and a personal appraisal of Harry. Armed with this information he made a successful appeal.

In "Balus bilong mipela", the story of MAF Australia and New Zealand, Vic Ambrose wrote:

Encouraged by the Melbourne Bible Institute's Principal, the Reverend John Searle, Harry shared his vision with others – ex-RAAF pilots, business and professional men, church leaders and students. A meeting was held in Melbourne on 30th June 1947 resulting in a resolution to form an autonomous body called "Missionary Aviation Fellowship" and to request affiliation with the Fellowships in England and America. Harry Hartwig was appointed the first full-time member of Australian MAF.

By 1951 Harry was able to take the first MAF aircraft to New Guinea, and commenced a programme of missionary flying. Only three months later he was killed in an air crash. New Guinea is one of the most difficult flying areas in the world; flying there will always be fraught with a certain amount of risk. Harry Hartwig, pioneer MAF New Guinea pilot, underlined this truth with his life.

At the time of writing, MAF Australia has been having a series of celebrations marking their fifty years of service. From one aircraft in 1951 there are now over fifty aircraft in Papua New Guinea, Australia and Cambodia. From two families in 1951, there are now two-hundred-and-fifty family units serving with MAF in those countries.

British MAF had similar small beginnings, and also suffered a crash in their first aircraft, though fortunately without loss of life. As Stuart King put it:

In Bangladesh an amphibian Beaver aircraft is used to convey patients and staff to the floating hospital and medical centres.

"While Murray Kendon had been patrolling the Atlantic, Jack Hemmings had been flying with the Air Force in India, and I had been an engineering officer with an RAF squadron in Europe. In those days we were both far too busy to look beyond our immediate futures. But neither of us was to remain long untouched by Murray's ideas."

Jack Hemmings was at school with me at Christ's Hospital, and we were to meet again in India in 1945 when we found ourselves sharing an RAF truck taking us from the airfield at Mauripur (Karachi) to the crew transit billets. Without knowing it, we had landed within a few minutes of each other, I in my Liberator from England, while Jack had flown a Dakota on an internal flight in India. Though by then I had heard from Trevor Strong and Murray Kendon, I little knew that Jack was to become British MAF's first full-time pilot.

From its early beginnings the work grew, and in 1995, what

is now MAF Europe, celebrated fifty years of existence. By then it was operating from bases in seven African countries, flying into a further twelve with a total of thirty-one aircraft. Subsequently work opened up in Mongolia, and now, including MAF/USA, nearly two hundred aircraft operate worldwide in more than thirty countries. On average every four minutes an MAF aircraft takes off somewhere in the world. In recent refugee crises in Africa all the main aid agencies have used MAF aircraft (fixed wing and helicopter) to get into and out of various refugee centres. In the spring of 2000, seventeen MAF aircraft were used to assist relief work during the Mozambique floods.

Operationally, MAF/Europe, MAF/USA and MAF/Australia and New Zealand remain separate organisations, and by and large each operates in particular areas of the world. MAF/USA

Malambo is in one of the remote areas of Tanzania regularly visited by MAF aircraft.

started (and continues) in Central and South America. Many will remember the dramatic story of the 'Mid-Century Martyrs', the five missionaries (including MAF pilot Nate Saint) who were murdered by the Auca Indians in 1956 – a story that inspired many to join MAF. Now MAF/USA (by far the largest numerically) operates also in a number of countries in Africa and the Far East. From time to time there have been loans and/or exchanges of personnel and aircraft between the three organisations. David Marfleet, for instance, who trained as a helicopter pilot with the British Army, flew both helicopters and Cessnas with MAF/USA for some years in Irian Jaya, formerly Dutch New Guinea. Helicopters are far more expensive to operate than fixed-wing aircraft, and so are only used in areas where the provision of airstrips is impractical. David Marfleet's biography, "Wings like Eagles", written by Clive Langmead was published by Lion Publishing plc in 1991.

In recent years, the term "missionary" has become politically unacceptable in some countries. Firstly, MAF/USA, then MAF Europe and finally MAF Australia and New Zealand have adopted the shortened title "Mission Aviation Fellowship".

Chapter 11

Out of the RAF –
but not finished with flying

In 1946, demobbed from the RAF with the rank of Flying Officer, I was torn between my love of flying and furthering my career. It appeared I had five options ahead of me:

My commanding officer was trying to persuade me to apply for a permanent commission in the RAF; my best friend on the Squadron was studying with a view to joining what was then British European Airways; MAF was just starting up; my dear aunt and Godmother who loved me greatly was keen for me to apply for a grant to do teacher training; and, finally, the Telephone Service was holding my job for me.

The permanent commission tempted me, but after five years in uniform, I felt it was time to return to civilian life. Civilian flying also held attractions. However having been on the transport job to India for the last eighteen months, I was somewhat fed up with existing out of a suitcase.

MAF had its attractions, but in the early days and to some extent even now, pilots also had to be fully qualified engineers, which I was not. Moreover, I was never good at languages, a necessity if flying in remote parts of the world.

Teacher training had never stood a chance, since when I was at school I had made up my mind I could never be a teacher; I still can recollect the dance we led some of them who were not adept at keeping control.

The Telephone Service had been fair in not only holding my

job, but had made up my salary during my first months in the RAF when my weekly pay was tuppence ha'penny. So I felt a moral obligation to return to them, and with no strong leanings to go elsewhere, I resumed my former career.

I was very fortunate when rejoining the Telephone Service. During the war there were no promotion exams, and selection was solely by interview. Again to be fair, they offered interviews to ex-service personnel, so I applied. Out of 880 applications nationally, I was offered one of the 24 posts, following three interviews successively at area, regional and national headquarters. Certain technical criteria concerning the number of City and Guilds certificates had to be met, I had obtained just enough to qualify. So I was able to take up an administrative post without the necessity of struggling through any more exams.

I continued in my old job for six months whilst all the interviews progressed, being twenty-seven by the time I joined the training course in London. Rejoicing in the title of Assistant Traffic Superintendent, I worked in the south eastern area of the metropolis for a number of months. Then I successfully applied for a post in Post Office Headquarters in St. Martin's-le-Grande where I worked for seven years, travelling daily from Wallington.

You will recall that in 1944, I had spent a brief time at RAF Aldergrove, Northern Ireland while on the Liberator Conversion Course, and that it was there that John Johnston, my Navigator, introduced me to two of the Crawford sisters. One of them, Betty, became friendly with my dear aunt in Wallington, and corresponded with her from time to time.

Shortly after the war Betty came over to her cousin's wedding in Bournemouth, advising my aunt of her impending arrival. My aunt told me, and the two of us met. One thing led to another and, as they say, we "hit it off" and became engaged. I proposed on Box Hill and travelled to Northern Ireland for Christmas 1949 to seek her father's permission. We were married in June 1950 at the Presbyterian Church in Glenarm, and

Our wedding day, Glenarm, 1st June 1950

spent our honeymoon at one of my favourite holiday spots, Tre-arddur Bay in Anglesey.

In the mid-thirties, after his parents moved to a nursing home where they spent their last years, my father had the Wallington house divided into two flats. The ground-floor flat was let to various tenants during the war, but was fortunately available in 1950, and became our first home. We attended the Parish Church at the end of our road, where I had been confirmed, and was appointed a sidesman. Betty joined the Young Wives' group, and was also diligent in rounding up a number of local children and taking them to Sunday School. One friend, now grown-up and with children of his own, recently told Betty that he owed his Christian convictions to the Sunday School to which she took him.

I had left the full-time Air Force in September 1946 and had not flown for some three years, when walking across London Bridge on my way to work during the glorious summer of 1949, I was attracted by the sound of an aircraft droning across the sky. The old urge returned and, as luck would have it, I bumped into someone with whom I had trained in Pensacola. We reminisced, I mentioning my nostalgia for flying. "Why not join the Reserve," he retorted, "I have and I go flying every weekend." Well, this was music to my ears, and in due course I did join the RAF Reserve with my old rank of Flying Officer. Redhill was my local base where once again I flew Tiger Moths and, a little later, Chipmunks.

Now thereby hangs a tale. The Chipmunk Mark 1 had a regrettable tendency for being difficult to recover from a spin. I cannot recall being warned about it, though it most certainly was a problem as modifications were later made to the tail, which improved matters. The Tiger Moth on the other hand, was so docile that all one had to do to stop it spinning was to let go of the controls. Too many hours in Tiger Moths had evidently made me careless.

In those days, the Reserve simply comprised pilots flying to

Chipmunks at Redhill, 1952

keep their hand in. Young lads from the ATC (Air Training Corps) would regularly ask for lifts and, provided their parents signed what we termed a "blood chit", exonerating the RAF in the event of a mishap, then we were happy to give them some air experience.

One Saturday morning, just after we started flying Chipmunks, a lad came across and asked if he might go up with me. I took him up and tried to give him some basic flying tuition, in the hope that the encouragement might eventually lead to a career in aviation. This lad was interested only in aerobatics, about which I was never all that keen, although I had performed them in training. As I remarked once before, Liberators do not fly too well upside down! Anyway we went through the repertoire, landed, and I went for lunch.

Resuming flying during the afternoon the same chap rolled up again, clearly a glutton for punishment. Once more I tried to persuade him to handle the controls, again with little success.

"Can I have some more aerobatics, Sir?" So I thought "Right, you have asked for it." Up we went to 7000 feet, and I put that Chipmunk through every stunt I could think of, culminating with a spin down to about 4000 feet. At this height, I tried to recover but it would not come out, simply went on spinning. I was very scared and, had I been alone, would probably have bailed out, but thinking the boy would freeze up, I could hardly leave him. I prayed hard and made one final violent attempt to stop it spinning. In my last desperate attempt, I kicked the opposite rudder with all my strength, and thrust the stick forward as hard as I could, and this worked. The spinning stopped, and I pulled out of the dive at 2000 feet above ground.

Shaking like a leaf, I flew back to the airfield and landed, taxied in and switched off. As he started climbing out I steadied my trembling hands and enquired of him, "Did you enjoy that?" "Yes Sir! Especially the aerobatics, Sir!"

Around 1953, the RAF decided that those of us who had fought in the last conflict were getting too long in the tooth to be any material use to them in any future war, so the RAF Reserve folded up. I still loved flying and, of course, was interested in MAF as well. I decided to take out a private pilot's licence while I still had the necessary recent flying experience; exams had to be passed in aviation law, navigation, and air-traffic control, but these were fairly routine. I obtained a private pilot's licence and joined the Surrey Flying Club based at Croydon aerodrome – now a housing estate. There was an annual membership subscription, after which I had to pay £3.15.0 (£3.75) per hour to hire an aircraft – this seemed a great deal of money at the time, and made me feel guilty spending it purely for my own enjoyment.

As I was helping to run the Crusader (Bible) class in Wallington, I decided to organise a recruiting competition. So I promised a flight as a prize to the lad who recruited the most new boys over a period of some nine months. Bob Hedderly, grandson of the senior leader, made up his mind that he was

Chipmunk airborne over Surrey, 1953

going to win. I had imposed strict rules on the competition. There was no question of bribing somebody in your class at school to come along for two or three Sundays, then claim him as a new boy. The visitor had to attend for ten consecutive Sundays, the requirement to earn his own Crusader badge; only then would he count as a recruit. Bob got nine of his mates to join the Crusaders, so, at the age of twelve, I gave him his first flight in a Hornet Moth, a two-seater side-by-side biplane.

In 1956 I passed a Post Office promotion board and requested provincial experience, suspecting that if I remained in London I would be stuck at HQ for the rest of my career. Manchester was my first choice, being halfway to Belfast and Betty's family home, and also because an old school friend, John Hansford, had kindly offered me lodgings until we could get our own home. The interview boards passed what they hoped would be a panel to last them for two years. I was way down the senior-ity ranking and reckoned it would be around eighteen months before I obtained a post. However, I was the only appointee to put Manchester as first choice, such being its popularity, or lack

Bob Hedderly's first (prize) flight, Hornet Moth, 29 October 1954

of it, at the time. There were, in fact, two vacancies in Manchester so I found myself winging north within weeks.

So, on arrival, I stayed with John and Dorothy Hansford and their four delightful children – a fifth was born a few months later. It was a little difficult to find a suitable property to buy at a price we could afford. To make hunting easier, Betty joined me from Wallington, and we moved into a nearby rented flat on 1st January 1957. John was Churchwarden at St. Edmund's, a vast Victorian church in Whalley Range. We found ourselves part of the same congregation, eventually buying a house on the edge of the parish. When John moved away in 1960, on becoming Headmaster of Bury Grammar School, I succeeded him as Churchwarden, remaining so until we ourselves moved on in 1976. Once again Betty became involved with Sunday School, in charge of the youngest class, known to her as the "wee tinies". She, herself, became known as "Auntie Betty" to all the children of the Church.

This was the era of "Fact and Faith" 16mm high-quality colour films, produced by the Moody Institute of Science and Technology in Chicago, and much appreciated by churches and educational establishments. After a brief course, I became one of several projectionists showing these films in a number of venues over the Greater Manchester area – sometimes alone, sometimes with an assistant. I still have vivid memories of the time we were asked to show a film at a Christmas party arranged for elderly folk by a South Manchester church. My friend, Brian Cheal, and I had set up the projector in an adjacent room, but it would not start despite all our efforts. "I hope you're praying," I said to Brian. "Yes – Lord, please send an electrician," he replied. Within seconds in walked a church member to enquire if we were ready. "Could you use a meter?", he asked when we had explained our dilemma, "my house is just down the road." We soon found there was a broken wire in a 7-way connector, and bypassing it with a length of flex, we were away!

One year Ian Cory, Scripture Union representative in the Manchester area, devised a multi-media presentation that he called a "Think-Through" – an evangelistic effort using music, film, drama and testimony. The music was by the "Glorylanders", four lads who had a very attractive repertoire of songs. Drama came in the form of the interview with Mary Magdalene from Stuart Jackman's novel "The Davidson Affair", and to illustrate particular points I showed extracts from the Fact and Faith films – "God of the Atom" and "Signposts Aloft". The latter contains the story of the "Lady Be Good", the American Liberator bomber that disappeared on the way back to North Africa after a bombing raid over Italy in April 1943, and was only discovered 15 years later in the desert. It is a vivid example of how an airman needs to trust his instruments, as the crew had passed over their base believing that they were still far out in the Mediterranean, and so assumed their instruments were faulty. At the end of the extract, Ian told the audience that a Liberator pilot was present, and called me out to quiz me about my faith and wartime experiences.

In the course of a few months we took the presentation to 30 venues from Manchester, Liverpool and Chester, right up to Edinburgh and Glasgow. My outstanding recollection of this tour stems from the prayer meetings we had before each "performance" – the Glorylanders in particular were an inspiration to know and share with. One less pleasant recollection is that lugging two 16mm projectors about resulted in a spell in Salford Hospital to have a hernia repair.

Shortly after our move to Manchester, Bob Hedderly came to the city as a student. In fact he was in digs with us for his first term, being unable to get into a hall of residence. He joined the University Air Squadron out at Woodvale, learning to fly there. By then I was flying at Woodvale and it just so happened that I was in the air when he went out on his first solo. I heard his instructor call up the tower, and I watched him complete his first lone flight – from above.

Bob finished his building degree, returning home for a time where he joined his local flying club, meantime saving every penny he could. After three years, he gave up his job and paid for himself to be trained as a flying instructor. Having qualified, he obtained a position as an instructor at Denham Airport for a few years until he was sufficiently qualified to apply to, and be accepted by, MAF. For seven years he flew in Ethiopia until MAF was expelled, following the deposition of Haile Selassie by the communists. He then returned home, and is to this day a commercial airline pilot.

In 1993 the present Ethiopian government invited MAF back, but withdrew their licence a couple of years later. However an Ethiopian former MAF pilot, Solomon Gizaw, has set up Abyssinian Flight Services to operate a charter service.

Solomon has kept the vision for helping isolated missions as well as aid agencies.

After fifty-four years of marriage, I realise how much I owe to Betty's care and capability for so much of that time. She had a deserved reputation as cook and baker and loved to entertain. Her cakes were eagerly sought after at all the church sales. In all our homes we had guests to stay, and visitors were always very welcome. In Manchester there were lots of single folk such as students and teachers who were living away from home. Sunday nights saw up to a dozen of these entertained after evening service to a good supper, a sing around the piano and a thought-provoking epilogue. The friendships we made during those days have been lasting, as has been demonstrated so enthusiastically by those who returned in turn to celebrate our Silver, Ruby and Golden Weddings. Two in particular have shown their love by their practical concern for us in the recent more difficult days.

Betty had three sisters, each with four children. In the late 1960s, Maureen, the youngest, who lived on the family farm, developed a tumour on the spine, which rendered her paralysed from the neck down. At the time, her eldest child was only twelve and the youngest six. Betty went over to Ireland to look after the children and hold the family together, staying almost full-time for nearly three years. If we had been granted children of our own, this would not have been possible. While Betty was away I lived alone and flew across for a long weekend about every six weeks. Maureen was originally given only three months to live but in the end it was sixteen years before she was finally taken from us. In spite of many prayers, no physical cure took place, yet her spirit was so wonderfully healed that she was a blessing to all who visited and/or attended her.

Though I had been deterred from joining MAF at the start, I was not going to be allowed to forget this work, and two further links were made in the 1960s. Among the young people entertained in our home in Manchester was an Australian,

Heather Langmead, in England for twelve months looking after the children of a couple on attachment to Manchester University. Feeling rather homesick, she was particularly attracted to Betty who reminded her of her own mother. Photographs confirm the likeness. As a result she became a very close friend, visiting us regularly on her days off. At the end of her time in England, she broke her journey back to Australia in Papua New Guinea, where she met up with, and became engaged to Alan Stray, who just happened to be a MAF pilot. We have retained links with Alan and Heather over the years; they and their children have visited us, as have also Harry Hartwig's widow Margaret, now married to Dr Rob Baldock, so we have been kept abreast of all the activities of MAF Australia and New Zealand.

It was at an Easter house party run by Crusaders in the Manchester area that I met Tom Frank, then a student at Manchester University, learning to fly with the University Air Squadron, with his sights set on a future with MAF. After gaining experience as an instructor, he flew for MAF in Ethiopia just before the period when Bob Hedderly was there. He used to send me back sets of slides, accompanied by a tape on which he graphically described his attempts at learning Amharic.

Later Tom returned to England and was for a time General Secretary of MAF/UK at their then headquarters in North London. He became concerned at the expense of bringing down to London enquiring candidates who were not necessarily suitable MAF material. Would I consider giving preliminary interviews to applicants from the north of England and recommending or otherwise further interviews in London? I agreed and saw a few, the most notable being Wesley Gibson who served MAF as an engineer for some years.

Tom also told me of his vision to set up a network of MAF local representatives who might assist him in making the work known in their part of the country. In due course this came to pass, and I became the first of MAF's Area Representatives. My "patch" covered the North West of England and involved speaking to church organisations, schools and a number of secular organisations such as Probus clubs – indeed any other interested party. Originally we were supplied with filmstrips and more recently videos of which I still maintain a library of eight or nine. Over more than twenty years I have taken between three- and four-hundred deputations. I also helped staff the MAF display stand at the Keswick Convention for a number of years. Betty was always a great help at these deputations. While I took the formal part of each meeting, she exercised her skills in making conversation over the refreshments that followed.

It has been difficult to assess the success of these activities, though generally I have been received with enthusiasm and sometimes invited back to the same venues on an annual or occasional basis. Occasionally there have been particular encouragements, such as when David Staveley, MAF's Flight Safety Officer, told me in a letter that my showing of the Mid-Century Martyrs filmstrip at the Crusader Camp when he was a seventeen year old junior officer, was one of the links in the chain that brought him into MAF.

I also learnt a lesson not to write off as useless any apparent failures. The Christian deputy head of a girls' school in the Lake District invited me on a number of occasions to address their Sunday morning service. This was a compulsory "parade" for the two-hundred-and-fifty boarders. They filed in and sat expressionless, apparently quite disinterested in anything spiritual let alone missionary. Much later, I was to hear that one of those girls had a conversion experience years afterwards that led her to give up her job and go to Bible School. Towards the end of her course she was praying to be shown what God wanted her to do and, leafing through a Christian magazine, came across a MAF advertisement for aircraft engineers. Immediately her mind went back to the MAF filmstrip I had shown at her school all those years before. She felt that this was what she was being directed to do. And so, after a long training course in America – the only girl among more than thirty men – she qualified as an aircraft maintenance engineer. Anne Lawson has been serving MAF in Tanzania for the past six years. "You started all this", she exclaimed when she came as a candidate to an MAF conference we attended.

There was no way I was going to relinquish flying simply through having moved north into Lancashire. I transferred my club membership to The Lancashire Aero Club flying from Barton near Manchester. There I flew for the first time an Auster in which I gave many people their first taste of flying. Aerobatics did not figure largely in my repertoire mainly due to the chronic lack of power of the Auster, it being so underpowered compared to all the RAF planes I had flown. It seemed it would never get off the ground, though it was fine once you got it airborne.

I enjoyed my flying from Barton, but then got wind of an appeal for pilots to become staff pilots at Woodvale aerodrome near Southport, giving air experience to ATC lads. So I applied, was successful and recommissioned as a Flying Officer. I did five years at Woodvale during which time my promotion to Flight Lieutenant came through. This was an automatic promotion based on my years of service as a Flying Officer. My commitment at Woodvale was to attend on two days per month, and in general I achieved this by flying every other Saturday. In addition we had the opportunity to provide air experience for cadets at Easter and Summer camps, which were held at various operational airfields, and were of one or two weeks' duration. In all, I attended seven of these camps: four at Easter and three in the summer.

One of the latter was a two-week spell at Valley, flying Tiger Moths. These aircraft had no radios, so we were only allowed to fly after 6.00 pm in the evenings, when the jet trainers had finished for the day. (Betty had come with me and we were staying with an uncle and aunt of mine nearby, so we spent all

George R.

George VI *by the Grace of God,* OF GREAT BRITAIN, IRELAND AND THE BRITISH DOMINIONS BEYOND THE SEAS, KING, DEFENDER OF THE FAITH, &c.

To Our Trusty and well beloved John James Vladimir Glazebrook, D.F.C. Greeting:

WE, *reposing especial Trust and Confidence in your Loyalty, Courage, and good Conduct, do by these Presents Constitute and Appoint you to be an Officer in Our Royal Air Force Volunteer Reserve from the Twelfth day of October 1949. You are therefore carefully and diligently to discharge your Duty as such in the Rank of Flying Officer or in such other Rank as We may from time to time hereafter be pleased to promote or appoint you to and you are in such manner and on such occasions as may be prescribed by Us to exercise and well discipline in their duties such Officers, Airmen and Airwomen as may be placed under your orders from time to time and use your best endeavours to keep them in good Order and Discipline. And We do hereby Command them to Obey you as their superior Officer and you to Observe and follow such Orders and Directions as from time to time you shall receive from Us, or any superior Officer, according to the Rules and Discipline of War, in pursuance of the Trust hereby reposed in you.*

GIVEN at Our Court, at Saint James's the Fifteenth day of November 1949, in the Thirteenth Year of Our Reign

By His Majesty's Command

Recommissioning Certificate, RAFVR, 15 November 1949

day at the beach!) Valley airfield is on the north-western shore of the mainland of Anglesey, and taking off into the prevailing north-westerly wind we flew over a narrow strip of water and, still quite low, over the southern tip of Holyhead Island, where there was a family with about four children camping on a private estate. Every time they heard me approaching they would rush out and wave excitedly, and I would wave back. On my last visit to Valley I went down to the shore and found a boatman who rowed me across, so that I might go and meet this family. With great delight, they told me that they had always waved at aeroplanes, but this was the first time anyone had waved back! They called me "the wavy man" and were so pleased to meet me and persuaded me to stay for a meal.

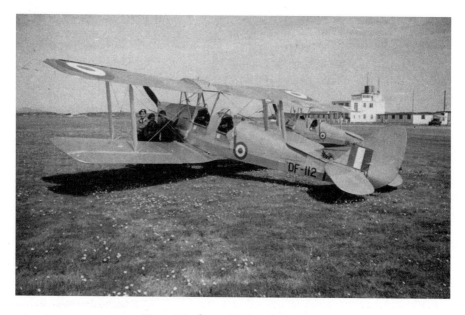

Tiger Moths at Valley, July 1953

My final official flight in charge of an RAF aircraft was during March 1965.

Chapter 12

My Last Years in the Telephone Service

Manchester was the North West Regional Headquarters of Post Office Telephones, and here I spent nineteen happy years before moving to Lancaster in 1975. By now, having only seven years to retirement, I was looking forward to unwinding and had very mixed feelings about moving, vividly recalling two episodes from my wartime experiences which left an indelible impression upon me.

The first concerned a great friend, Leslie Jones, like myself a Christian. We went through our training together at Pensacola on the Catalina Flying Boat. He was a little younger than I and was mad keen, as indeed were most of my generation, to be either a Hurricane or Spitfire pilot. I had accepted that whatever the powers that be wished me to do was right for me, but Leslie however went on determined to become a fighter pilot, being granted his wish on his seventh application. He, like me, had obtained his wings on the flying boat. He went back to England to join a Beaufighter Operational Training Unit. On a night exercise about three weeks into his course he crashed and was killed, never having seen active service.

The second such incident was when we were about to join Transport Command for the India run, which we were told would entail being away from base for around three weeks at a time. One of our number, whose name now eludes me, went to the CO saying that as he had just married, he really did not wish to be away for such long periods. Would it be possible to transfer to some other unit based in the UK? He was transferred to an Air Sea Rescue Unit flying Warwicks, a development of the Wellington which carried a lifeboat where the bomb bay had been located. They went out to look for a crew which had come down in the North Sea, and never returned.

So one chap had fought to get what he wanted. When he got it, it did him no good. Another tried to avoid doing something, and the alternative likewise proved fatal. This left me with a strong feeling that God knew what was best for me and I would accept it. When people advised me to apply for a job out at an area office, my attitude was one of "If it is offered to me or somebody wants to transfer me, then I will go, but I am not going to ask for it".

There was a vacancy in Preston for which folk tried unsuccessfully to get me to apply. Next there was one in Lancaster, which my boss encouraged me to go for. I did nothing. Weeks later he tackled me again, leaning on me quite heavily. My retort was that I would take it if offered. Eventually the post of Head of Customer Services was advertised nationally in the weekly Post Office Gazette. This meant that if I wanted it I had to put something on paper. Eventually I did. It read "I should like to apply for the vacancy in Lancaster advertised in the Post Office Gazette".

That, I thought, is the end of that, bearing in mind the post covered the whole of the Lake District, and I envisaged a queue a mile long. Weeks went by and I assumed my application had been unsuccessful. One afternoon my boss came into my office, sat down, discussed various aspects of business, got up to leave, went into the corridor, then put his head back round the door and remarked "By the way, keep quiet about it for now, but it's almost certain you have got Lancaster".

The date was 23rd June 1975, a blistering day. Betty was away visiting relations in Northern Ireland. I was very happy in Manchester, a Churchwarden and involved in all manner of activities. Lying alone in bed I mused, where do you start looking for a home and a church at the age of fifty-five? No way could I sleep. Being June it was light very early so I reached over to pick up my Daily Light from beside the bed. This is a series of Biblical quotes, a page for each day of the year. I looked up the text for 24th June. Part of it hit me between the eyes:

"The Lord went before them to search out a resting place for them".

I could hardly refuse now!

By 3rd November I was in post at Lancaster, though we still lacked a place to live, and had yet to sell our home in Manchester. I stayed with friends in Bare on the outskirts of Morecambe during the week, travelling home at weekends. We took the local papers every week, scanning them for suitable properties. Most were too expensive because Lancaster University had recently been established, thereby draining the stock of affordable housing. We had cleared the mortgage on our Manchester home and, bearing in mind my not-too-distant retirement, I did not wish to take on another. So our "top limit" was the price we were getting in Manchester, plus the very limited savings that we possessed.

Weeks went by, with Betty travelling north often on the Thursday so that we might view potential properties. While scanning the Westmorland Gazette, Betty spied an attractive property, though with no price quoted. We rang for details and sure enough it was too expensive, but the lady at the estate agency was quick off the mark and arranged to send details of further properties to my weekday address. In no time a wad of sale particulars arrived. By then I was wearying of the whole tiresome process, as trying to visualise a potential home in a foreign area is never easy. Eventually I did wade through them until my eye alighted on Waterside Cottage, Burton-in-

Lonsdale. Amazingly the price was right, the description was out of this world, as seemed Burton-in-Lonsdale itself.

Our church in Manchester had put us in touch with the local Vicar, Arthur Hughes, himself new to the area and residing at The Vicarage, Burton-in-Lonsdale. Arthur had no idea where Waterside Cottage was in his sprawling parish but very soon found out, and thought we should at least view it. I was still sceptical, the village being sixteen miles distant from Lancaster. I had been used to living only three miles from my office, and hoped that in Lancaster I might be able to pop home for lunch.

Arthur and his wife invited me to stay at the Vicarage while I viewed properties. It was now December and I have never been so cold as in that vast Victorian vicarage built at the behest of Thomas Thornton, an early millionaire who had also put up the money to build the Parish Church of All Saints in 1869. The first incumbent was the Reverend Frederick Binyon whose second son Laurence became immortalised with Remembrance Day services worldwide when he wrote "For the Fallen", with its poignant third verse commencing "They shall grow not old as we that are left grow old"! I just hope his early home was a little warmer than when I visited it. Arthur and his family only stuck it that first winter, after which a smaller more economical vicarage was found in the centre of the village.

Eventually we looked at Waterside Cottage, which certainly had some attractive features, but yet the travelling aspect was still bugging me. Back home in Manchester we puzzled over it for a couple more sleepless nights. The following Monday, Tuesday and Wednesday, I was on a training course down in Rugby staying at the Postal Management Training Centre. Monday evening found me pacing the streets of Rugby praying about this dilemma and wondering how on earth we should decide what to do. For the second time in my life I heard that voice which now said to me:

"You have been looking for a home and a church for eight months; here is a home and a church, now get on with it. "

I rang Betty from a call box in Rugby, recounting my experience and telling her that I did not see how I could say to the Almighty, "Look Lord, this is not quite what we wanted. Can you perhaps find us something a little nearer Lancaster?" She retorted that we ought to go and have a further look at the house, which is what we did. That effectively sealed it.

Having become members of the congregation of All Saints Church, I was astounded to learn of a coincidence relating back to my school days at Christ's Hospital. I have already mentioned the name Thornton in connection with building the church and vicarage. That was Thomas Thornton, nephew of Richard Thornton who was born the son of the local cobbler in Burton, living in a cottage on the site of which now stands the Parish Church.

Richard too had attended Christ's Hospital School circa 1780. It had been founded in 1552 by King Edward VI as a result of

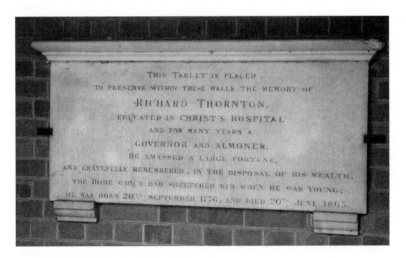

Memorial Plaque to Richard Thornton, Christ's Hospital Cloisters

hearing a sermon by Bishop Ridley on the abysmal state of the capital's children. He also founded St Bartholomew's and Bridewell as schools. The former became a hospital. Bridewell continued as a school and is now known as King Edward's School, Witley, in Surrey. Richard Thornton went on to a long action-packed life as a result of which when he died in 1865, he was the richest man in the country. He built and endowed the village school in Burton, which is to this day known as Richard Thornton's School.

When Christ's Hospital School moved out of London to Horsham in 1902, the new boarding houses were named after famous old boys. These included Charles Lamb, Taylor Coleridge and one Sir Edward Thornton, a distinguished diplomat of the early 1800s. He was not as far as I can ascertain related to Richard Thornton, but it was still a remarkable coincidence that when I was at Christ's Hospital, I was in one of the Thornton houses, little realising that I should end up in Richard's birthplace.

Within the Telephone Service I now held the rank of Chief Traffic Superintendent, effectively heading that side of the business in the Lancaster Telephone area. This did not involve, as might be supposed, the transport aspect of our business but rather the quality of service to our customers, including control of the operators and supervisors (day and night) at the six staffed exchanges in the Area – Lancaster; Kendal; Barrow in Furness; Penrith; Whitehaven and Carlisle. My main office was in Lancaster but I also had office staff in Carlisle. I had to visit all these units, in addition to dealing directly with some of our more difficult customers. One year I deputised for the Telephone Manager whenever he was absent.

The Telephone Service had started retiring folk at sixty, but there was no replacement for me so I soldiered on till I was nearly sixty-two, retiring on 30th September 1981; the very next day, the Telephone Service separated from the Post Office, and became the independent British Telecom.

Chapter 13

Camps, Holidays and Reunions

I mentioned earlier meeting Tom Frank at an Easter house party run by Manchester Area Crusaders. I attended ten of these Easter house parties in all, and for more than thirty years helped to run camps for Crusaders in the summer holidays. At Westbrook in the Isle of Wight, Crusaders own a property purchased shortly after WWII as a memorial to Crusaders who lost their lives in the war (one of whom was Jack Wallworth, a leader of the Wallington class). Here the boys (and their officers) sleep in tents in the grounds, but the house provides comfortable accommodation for meetings and meals, with modern kitchen facilities.

Some other venues were distinctly more primitive, and this was particularly true of Gomshall in Surrey, where Wallington Crusaders held their own camp over the Whitsun weekend for many years. Here Betty and two other ladies – Gwen Moxon and Molly Amos – laboured valiantly, doing all the cooking over a wood fire built in a trench and covered (when wet, which it frequently was!) only by a groundsheet spread over four poles.

Three of the summer camps were joint Crusader/MAF ventures, and were on an airfield with the youngsters being given the choice of parachute jumping, power flying or gliding. During these camps I did some power flying and also some gliding, but although I had been taught to use a parachute in an emergency, I saw no point in jumping out of a perfectly good aeroplane! I had not tried a glider before but eventually was

MAF Cessna 180. MAF/Crusaders Camp, Headcorn, August 1981

Bergfalke Glider – first solo, Eaglescott airfield, August 1986

allowed to go solo in one. This was the first time that I had been up alone in the air for some twenty years. The venue was a private airfield in North Devon, Eaglescott, and the date 12th August 1986. The Glorious Twelfth!

In addition to pure gliders, they had on the airfield a powered glider. The small engine was used for take off after which it was switched off. The Crusaders had paid for one flight for each member of the camp, including myself, though I was last up. The instructor was young, very surly, non-committal, barely speaking. He took off, climbed to 2000 feet and switched off the engine. I was invited to "have a go", which I did with relish.

I turned downwind; he told me when to turn across, and when to put on the air brakes as we made the final approach and I landed it. The instructor started the engine again; I taxied round to the dispersal and he switched off. He lifted the hatch, I said, "Thank you, I enjoyed that!", but he stomped off to the instructors' room without a word.

Later I learned what then transpired. Bursting in he announced, "That man can fly!" The chief instructor looked up and remarked, "He's only got five times as many hours as you". "Why didn't you tell me?" "I thought I'd let you find out!"

Over the years we have been fortunate with holidays. In 1955 we spent two weeks in the lovely country of Norway, with a party from the Post Office Christian Association. At Vos, we got to know a schoolmaster and some of the members of the School Christian Union, taking part in one of their meetings. As a result several young people visited us in Wallington and in Manchester, whilst on their Gap year in England; in 1972 we spent a month staying in the homes of four of our Norwegian friends from previous years.

The trip to the Pensacola reunion of 1982 gave us the chance to spend two days at the HQ of the American MAF at Redlands, California; during that month-long trip we also visited relations and friends in Canada. Five years later, we returned to Canada to celebrate the retirement of my cousin John Pelly. This magnificent extravaganza, kept secret until the last minute, was staged at his holiday home on an island in Lake Muskoka, Ontario, and on the RMS Segwun, the last coal-fired pleasure steamer on the Lakes. When he arrived by launch at the island, with his wife, son, brother and sister-in-law, he was staggered to find eighty of his friends and relations waiting to greet him!

About this time, an old school friend and his South African wife visited us whilst on a touring holiday. Geoff Corbin and I had not met in fifty years, yet we had so much in common that we were immediately drawn together. In spite of obvious differences of background, Esme and Betty got on well, too. Subsequently, Geoff and Esme came back to visit us on two further occasions, staying on the second visit for ten days, "On the strict understanding", said Geoff, when arranging the trip, "that we discuss a return match".

That "return match" took place in 1990, when as part of our Ruby Wedding celebrations, we flew to South Africa for a seven-week holiday based at their home in Somerset West. We had a long tour with them through other parts of the country, including a weekend in Lesotho, where we had friends who worked for the British Council. The MAF operated the Flying Doctor Service in Lesotho, and I arranged for the four of us to have a ninety-minutes' joyride around the country in one of their aircraft.

On the morning the flight was booked, the pilot, on his first trip of the day, reported that the weather was overcast and pretty rough; we might still go, though it was likely to be bumpy and not ideal for joyriding. Our friends rapidly lost interest, but I was not going to miss a chance to fly in a MAF aircraft; after all, I had flown in rough weather before! Betty, bless her, joined me; the pilot of the Cessna 206 decided that he would remove the couple of seats now vacant, and make the flight an operational one. This suited me all the better. We took off, flew around several bush airstrips and eventually landed on a tiny airstrip about 7000 feet up in the Drakensburg Mountains, where we unloaded all the stores for a medical centre.

As soon we had started to gain height on the return journey, the pilot asked me to take the controls while he completed his paperwork. Betty reckoned he was testing me out to see if I still knew what I was doing. He must have been satisfied, for he allowed me to fly it all the way back and then make the landing. That really made my weekend. Not bad for my seventy-first year! Now when people ask me whether I have flown an MAF aircraft in Africa, I can truthfully say "Yes – once!"

I still maintain my links with 206 Squadron, now based at RAF Kinloss and very much involved in maritime operations. They fly Nimrod Aircraft which are frequently used in SAR (search and rescue) missions around our shores and over the oceans, as are Sea King helicopters; these are regularly in the news either plucking survivors from some yachting mishap, or a wounded person after a mountain accident.

Sid Banks, of the Lancaster bombing fiasco, started his own business after the war, and has done rather well; he still flies his own aircraft, a four-seater monoplane. On several occasions he has flown this up to Kinloss for the Squadron reunions. We meet and greet on Friday evening, and on Saturday there is golf, a tour of the distilleries, or in the case of the ladies a shopping trip around one of the nearby towns; in the evening there is a grand dinner.

Neither Sid nor I were keen on any of the Saturday options so on no less than three occasions I have accompanied him on a flight around the Hebridean Islands. The first time, in 1989, Sid had brought along his own navigator and Betty made up a foursome. We were going to head for Benbecula, Sid offering me the controls for the flight out. We took off in bright sunlight climbing above clouds being blown in from the west, in due

206 Squadron reunion, Kinloss, 1989

course commencing a descent through them for the island run-way. At this stage the radios failed which meant that it was not safe to continue through the clouds so we climbed back up and returned home. The aircraft was too small to change seats so I flew there and back – a great thrill.

Another year we made a trip to Stornoway for lunch, and on the last occasion to Orkney, accompanied by the widow of our wartime Squadron Medical Officer who had a daughter living there. We lunched in Kirkwall. A great feeling to be up there again!

There is a chapel at RAF Kinloss near Forres where three stained-glass windows have been presented, each dedicated to one of the three resident squadrons. They feature in David Beaty's book "Light Perpetual", (*Airlife Publishing Ltd., 1995*) which tells the story of Aviators' Memorial Windows in places of worship throughout the United Kingdom.

That for 206 Squadron was designed by Brother Gregory Carling and Brother Michael de Klerk of Pluscarden Abbey, near Kinloss. Former members of the squadron were consulted as to whether it should feature a Fortress or Liberator. I gave

my vote for the latter, recounting in my letter that early frightening flight as a Liberator Captain. I never received an
acknowledgement, but when I arrived for the dedication cere-
mony in 1989, was amazed and delighted to find that not only
does the window feature a Liberator beneath the Squadron
motto Nihil Nos Effugit (Naught escapes us) but that at the top
of the window there is an extract from Psalm 139 "In the uttermost part of the sea, Thy hand will hold me".

It was in 1996 that we set off on our longest trip. In Australia,
I still have members of my wartime aircrew as well as acquain-
tances made through MAF, plus British relations and friends
who have emigrated there or to New Zealand. With the help of
some of these, we planned a round-the-world trip to visit as
many of them as possible. We flew from London via Los
Angeles, Honolulu and Fiji, where we had two restful days,
then on to New Zealand where we were met and entertained
by Gladys Shields (*née* Boyle), who had been Lady Worker at
our Manchester church.

Sadly, just one week later Betty suffered a serious brain
stroke. We had just spent one night with her cousin Carole
Crawford in Napier, and were due to drive on to stay with
Betty's niece Ruth Smith and her husband in Palmerston North.
Instead, Betty spent eight days in the hospital in Napier, and
Carole, bless her, looked after me and even lent me her car
every day to visit the hospital. The staff there were most helpful and gave me complete freedom to visit any time day or
night. On her release, Ruth and Andrew came up and drove us
to their home where we spent the greater part of the three
week's convalescence that the doctor had decreed. One day,
Murray and Minni Kendon drove over from Wellington and
had lunch with us; it was the first time Murray and I had met
since his visit to Oakington with Trevor Strong in 1945! Then
for 5 days other cousins Jim and Margaret Crawford looked
after us very kindly at their home in Hamilton before taking us
to Auckland, whence we were "medically repatriated" with an

escorting nurse direct to Manchester. Regretfully we never set foot in Australia. I had to be content with a glimpse of Sydney from 31,000 feet up on the flight deck of the 747.

At Manchester we were met by our old friends, Thain and Jean Flowers, who took us first to their own home, and after a couple of days helped us settle back in Burton-in-Lonsdale – and have been "keeping an eye on us" ever since!

Betty was very confused during those last weeks in New Zealand, and for quite a long time afterwards. Fortunately she remembers none of that now. But I am constantly thankful that the 'One who watches over me' provided me with so many helpful friends during that traumatic period.

Gradually over the months that followed things have improved, but compared with "pre-stroke" days, life was been very different. Betty is able to walk and talk, and reads a little but is not able to do much else without my assistance and encouragement. So, I am "head cook and bottle washer", and except for very short periods, am unable to leave her. For this reason, and under the guidance of our closest friends, we have moved to be near them in Cheshire.

We have much to be thankful for. We have always comple-mented each other, but while Betty had her independence, she did a great deal on her own – baking, visiting, and gardening, to name just a few. Now that she can do little without help we are drawn closer together, and thankfully, Betty is constantly grateful for the help I give her.

To return to my sister, Marietta; when I started work the short holidays with her and my mother stopped, and I was not to see her again for many years. I knew that she went into the RAF during the War, and also that she got married, but I did not even know her surname. My sister was always reckoned to take after mother, and myself after father; my loss of contact with her frankly did not worry me overmuch.

However, my sister, who had been seeking my whereabouts, but without success, was eventually rewarded. Some two or three years ago, my former school, Christ's Hospital, published "Who's Blue", listing former pupils and their careers, where known. A little later, she was talking to a neighbour of hers who had some connection with the school. She mentioned her long lost brother whereupon he produced the book and hey presto there was my name and address, history, the lot.

On my birthday, I received a letter and card from her, with the message, "This is the first birthday card you will have had from me in sixty years". She lives near Tintagel, in Cornwall, in what was bought as a holiday home, but then became their retirement base. When she became a widow, the rest of the family descended, including our late mother. The opportunity to meet her again, after sixty-five years, came when we were in the area for a Squadron Association reunion. Naturally, that meeting was emotional.

Many of the incidents recorded in this book are for various reasons indelibly etched into my memory. As I look back over life and what has been written, I am conscious that much has been omitted.

Bob Swallow, who did so much to get this book started, also coined the phrase that gave it its title. Certainly as I have recalled so many of the facts recorded here, the inference of a Divine Hand protecting and overruling in so many ways is undeniable. All of us, who lived through and survived the years of war, must admit that "but for the Grace of God" we might have been among the many thousands who lost their lives. Six thousand of those were Coastal Command aircrew, involved as I was in the Battle of the Atlantic, in which much larger numbers (73,000 Royal Navy men; 30,000 merchant seamen and 29,000 German U-boat crewmen) perished on and in those hostile waters.

For what purpose did I survive that dramatic Atlantic crossing in the troopship, escape the fate that overtook the Flight Lieutenant whose second pilot I had planned to be, avoid crashing into the island of Foula, and live through the hazards of enemy fire and the worst of the North Atlantic's winter weather? At least two of the finest Christians I met during the war were killed. I wonder if they were more ready for Heaven, while I still had much to learn.

Now in my eighty-fifth year, having moved from our home of twenty-five years in Burton-in-Lonsdale to a warden-controlled retirement development in Cheshire, I must confess myself at least semi-retired, though I have taken three local MAF deputations since coming to Knutsford, and have another booked for March 2005. As long as I remain fit I hold myself available, convinced that the One who watches over me will continue to do so.

Postscript from Bob Swallow

Fact they say is stranger than fiction. They might have added "and a darn sight more exciting". Jim's story epitomises this. There will be few who, having read of his exploits will not have been touched by his disarming candour, concern for others, and undoubted faith.

It has been both a pleasure and a trial to assist in writing his life story. A pleasure because Jim is a no-frills, no-graces, down-to-earth sort of person who describes the most hair-raising incidents in a matter-of-fact manner which leaves you gasping. A trial when you realise just how close to death he lived in a period of his life and how many of his friends paid the ultimate price.

For sure, there has been "Someone to watch over him."

List of Illustrations

Cover photographs

206 Squadron Liberator, June 1944 (see p.92)   Front cover

Jim and Betty Glazebrook   Back cover

206 Squadron Memorial Window, Chapel at
RAF Kinloss (see p.148)   Back cover

Jim Glazebrook DFC   Frontispiece

Photographs in the text

 1: Myself, aged 8, at Wallington   19
 2: Myself, aged 10, at Christ's Hospital   20
 3: My house – Thornton B, with Swimming Cup and
    Chess Shield, July 1934   21
 4: Thornton B Swimmers, July 1934, with Swimming
    Cup   22
 5: Part of the Course No. 30, No. 14 EFTS, Elmdon,
    November 1941   29
 6: With my first Instructor, P/O Andrews, Elmdon,
    November 1941   29
 7: Tiger Moth T 7222 – My first solo, 18th November, 1941   30
 8: Naval Aircraft N3N – the "Yellow Peril"   35
 9: Myself at Pensacola, June 1942   37
10: Building 624, the British Flight Battalion accommodation,
    Pensacola   37
11: "S-turns to Circles" – the circle we had to land in taken
    from 1000 feet, the point of engine cut   39
12: Three-plane formation – N3Ns   41
13: Three-plane formation – Kingfishers   41
14: Consolidated Catalina – PBY   42
15: Consolidated Sesqui-plane – P2Y   42
16: "Circuits and Splashes", Initial rush of water as throttles
    are opened   43

17: "Circuits and Splashes", Wake narrows as we get "on the step" 43

18: "Circuits and Splashes", End of wake shows point at which we're airborne 43

19: "Circuits and Splashes", Waterborne again 43

20: US Navy Pilot's qualification certificate, Nov. 1942 45

21: Aunt Katie and guests, last Sunday at Pensacola 46

22: Miss Kathlyn Monroe (Aunt Katie), June 1942 47

23: Memorial to Kathlyn Monroe, 1st Presbyterian Church, Pensacola (1981) 48

24: Sergeant Pilot Jim Glazebrook, November 1942 49

25: Sergeant Pilot Ken Graves, November 1942 49

26: The Instructors, Pensacola Flying Boat Squadron 49

27: John and Jim leaving Moncton, April 1943 51

28: I am dwarfed by the engine that pulled us to New York 51

29: John, on the engine that pulled us to New York 52

30: B25 – Mitchell 53

31: Avro Anson over the frozen St Lawrence River, January 1943 54

32: Avro Anson flight deck 54

33: My first crew – Back row: Draper, Meaker, MacManus, McCrostie and Clegg; Front row: Johnston, Glazebrook and Simpkin 55

34: My first crew – Fred, self and John 55

35: John and I dressed up to meet the Duke and Duchess of Windsor 57

36: Sir Walter Moore, Deputy Governor of the Bahamas 57

37: B24 – Liberator 58

38: Liberator instrument panel 58

39: Fortress FL450 at Benbecula 67

40: Lagens Airfield, Azores – General View 73

41: Lagens Airfield, Azores – Tented Billets 74

42: Lagens Airfield, Azores – Laying the metal strip runway 74

43: Fortress R/206 after the attack on U-575 78

44: Lagens Airfield, Azores: Draper, Johnston, Beaty, Glazebrook, MacManus, Meaker and Cunningham 78

45: Fl. Lt. Beaty and Fl. Lt. Hart and their crews. Fortress training, Thornaby-on-Tees, September 1943 79

46: My crew at Leuchars, August 1944. Back row: Boorman, Nicholson, Glazebrook, Ellison and Bain; Front Row: Hartwig, Riley, Angel, Smith and McLean 84
47: Liberator over Trevose Head, June 1944 92
48: The Leigh Light installed under a Liberator's starboard wing 94
49: Liberator L/206 off the Scottish Coast, March 1945 100
50: Surrendering U-boat, U-1231, 13th May, 1945 101
51: Keith Jones, Chief Executive of MAF/UK 111
52: Maasai mother and baby beneath the wing of MAF Cessna at Malam 112
53: The arrival of the plane is always greeted with enthusiasm 113
54: Christian Blind Mission using MAF to carry teams 114
55: A Cessna Caravan aircraft in Madagascar 114
56: Harry Hartwig at my aunt's home, "Barn Mead", Ingatestone 116
57: MAF amphibian Beaver aircraft in Bangladesh 118
58: MAF at Malambo, Tanzania 119
59: Our Wedding Day, Glenarm, 1st June, 1950 123
60: Chipmunks at Redhill, 1952 125
61: Chipmunk airborne over Surrey, 1953 127
62: Bob Hedderly's first (prize) flight, Hornet Moth, 29 October 1954 128
63: Recommissioning Certificate, RAFVR, 15th November 1949 135
64: Tiger Moths at Valley, July 1953 136
65: Memorial Plaque to Richard Thornton, Christ's Hospital Cloisters 141
66: MAF Cessna 180. MAF/Crusaders Camp, Headcorn, August 1981 144
67: Bergfalke Glider – first solo, Eaglescott airfield, August 1986 144
68: 206 Squadron reunion, Kinloss, 1989 148

Bibliography

The life of John Fletcher, in *A History of the English Church, Vol. VII,* Overton and Relton, published by Macmillan, 1906

War History of 206 Squadron, J.J.V. Glazebrook, published by 206 Squadron, 1946

On Wings of Love, Lee Roddy, published by Thomas Nelson, 1981

Men of Coastal Command, 1939-1945, Chaz Bowyer, published by William Kimber, 1985

Balus Bilong Mipela (the story of the Missionary Aviation Fellowship Australia and New Zealand), Vic Ambrose, published by MAF Melbourne, 1987

The Condor of the Andes, C.P. Wagner and S. McCullogh, published by Evangelistic Literature Enterprise, 1987

Flying for God, Harold Morton, published by Bio Kingdom Enterprises

Wings like Eagles, Clive Langmead, published by Lion, 1991

Hope has Wings, Stuart King, published by Marshall Pickering, 1993

Light Perpetual, David Beaty, published by Airlife Publishing, 1995

Winged Life, Betty Campbell Beaty, published by Airlife Publishing, 2001

Index

Aldergrove 66, 82, 122
Ambrose, Vic 15,117
Amos, Molly 143
Andrews, P/O 30
Angel, Sgt Frank 88, 105
Anson 50, 64, 65
Aquitania, 55 63
Arnhem 115
Auster 134

B/206 95
Baldock, Dr Rob 132
Baldock, Margaret 15
Balfour, Rt Hon Harold
  69
Ballykelly 103, 104
Banff 98
Banks, Sid 98, 147
Bare, Morecambe 139
Barker, W/C 104
Barton 134
Beaty, Betty Campbell
  14, 98
Beaty, David 14, 63, 64,
  75, 76, 77, 79, 80, 82,
  83, 97, 98, 99, 148
Beaufighter 63, 137
Beechcraft 115
Benbecula 68, 69, 147
Biddell, F/L Bill 65
Binyon, Laurence 140
Binyon, Rev. Frederick
  140
Bircham Newton 66, 81
Birkenhead 101
Birmingham, Al 36
Bordeaux 65
Bowyer, Chaz 88

Bremen 67
Brice, Mrs 61–2
Brogue 80
Brunsbuttel 65
Burton-in-Lonsdale 11,
  139, 140, 141, 150,
  152

Cairo 104
Candy, W/C CD 66
Carling, Brother Gregory
  148
Carlisle, F/O 91
Carlson, Paul 115
Castel Benito 104, 106
Caswell, John 14
Catalina, PBY 40, 43, 70,
  137
Caulfield, LAC Walter 65
Cessna 115, 120, 146
Charlottetown, PEI 50
Cheal, Brian 129
Chipmunk 124-126
Chisholm, G/C 108
Christ's Hospital 19, 20,
  21, 23, 24, 59, 61, 107,
  118, 141, 142, 151
Churchill, Winston 72
Cincinnati 36
Coleridge, Taylor 142
Conway, Sgt 93
Cooke, W/C 67
Corbin, Esme 146
Corbin, Geoff 146
Cory, Ian 129, 130
Crawford, Betty 122,
  124, 127, 128
Crawford, Carole 149

Crawford, Jim 149
Crawford, Margaret 149
Crawford, Maureen 131
Croydon 24
Croydon Aerodrome 19,
  126

D/206 95
Dakota 118
Dart, Ken 61
De Clerk, Brother
  Michael 148
Deighton, LAC 66
Denham 130
Detroit 34
Deverill, Sgt 66
Dover 64
Dublin 108
Dundee 83, 94, 95, 102
Dunkirk 64,65
Dunnet Head 86

Edward VI, HRH 141
Ellison, Sgt 99
Elmdon, 14 EFTS 28, 31
Everett, Marietta 150

Fairchild 24 115
Fisk, George 115
Fletcher, John 23, 24
Flowers, Jean 14, 150
Flowers, Thain 14, 150
Fortress 63, 64, 68, 69,
  70, 71, 73, 75, 76, 79,
  81, 148
Frank, Tom 132, 143
Freeman, LAC 65
Frost, F/O 92, 93, 102

Gibraltar 75
Gibson, Wesley 132
Gipsy Moth 115
Gizaw, Solomon 130, 131
Glazebrook, Rev James 24
Glenarm 52, 82, 122
Glorylanders, The 130
Gollan, F/S 93
Gourock 31
Graham, S/L. 95
Graves, Ken 32, 83
Greene, Betty 115
Griggs, Jack 27
Grosse Ile 34, 36, 37

Haggas, F/L 95
Haile Selassie 130
Halifax 98
Halifax, NS 33
Hampden 70
Hancock, F/L John 90
Hansford, Dorothy 128
Hansford, John 127, 128
Harper, S/L 95
Harris, Bert 67
Harrogate 63
Hartwig, F/S 'Harry' 83, 116, 117, 132
Harvard 40
Haverfield, destroyer 80
Heaton Park 31, 31
Hedderly, Bob 126, 130, 132
Hedderly, HV 23
Hemmings, Jack 118
Hendon 19
Herron, 'Wally' 115
Herron, Robert 115
Hobson, destroyer 80
Holmes, S/L JA 70
Holyhead 108
Hornet Moth 127

Horsham 19, 142
Hubbard, F/S 68
Hudson 65, 66, 67, 73
Hughes, Rev Arthur 140
Hurricane 137

Imperial Airways 19
Irian Jaya 120

Jackman, Stuart 129
Johnston, John 52, 60, 82, 122
Jones, Keith 15
Jones, Leslie 50, 137

Kean, P/O RT 65, 66
Keil 65,100
Kendon, Murray 112, 113, 115, 118, 149
Kennan, P/O Terry 66
King, Stuart 15,112, 117
King's Lynn 81
Kingfisher 40
Kinloss 147, 148
Knutsford 152

Lagens 72, 75
Lake Muskoka 146
Lamb, Charles 142
Lancaster (plane) 103,110,147
Lancaster (city) 137, 138, 139, 141, 142
Lang, Dr CS 22
Langford-Smith, Keith 115
Langmead, Clive 120
Langmead, Heather 132
Lawson, Anne 134
Leigh, W/C 94
Lesotho 146
Leuchars 83, 88, 95, 101, 102, 103, 104

Liberator 50, 53, 61, 62, 63, 81, 82, 83, 84, 86, 87, 90, 92, 96, 98, 99, 100, 103, 105, 118, 122, 129, 130, 148, 149
Liverpool 63,130
London 25,142
Longtown 64
Louisville 36

Madeley 23, 24
Manchester 31, 31, 127. 130, 137, 139, 140, 143, 145, 150
Marfleet, David 120
Mauripur, Karachi 118
McGowan, Helen 14
Melsbroek 104,105
Mellis, Charles 115
Messerschmitt 109 65, 66
Messerschmitt 110 92, 102
Miami 52, 53, 63
Midsomer Norton 17, 18
Milne, AA 20
Mitcham 26
Mitchell 53, 56, 59, 62
Mitchener, F/S 75
Moncton, NB 33, 50
Monroe, Kathlyn 46,47
Montcalm, SS 31
Montgomery, Al 36
Montreal 34
Moore, F/O 82
Moore, Sir Walter 60
Moxon, Gwen 143

N3N 35, 36, 38, 40
Narvik 96
Nashville 36
Nassau, Bahamas 60, 61
New York 61, 63
Nicholson, F/S JA 93

Nimrod 147
Normandy 27
North Coates 67

Oakington 104, 108–112, 149
Owen, F/O 68
Oxford (plane) 108
Oxford (city) 27

P2Y 43
Paignton, 4 ITW 28, 32
Parrott, Grady 115
Patrick, S/L 69
Pearce, F/L 101
Pearl Harbour 31
Pelly, John 146
Pembroke Dock 31
Pensacola 33, 36, 37, 43, 44, 46, 48, 56, 115, 124, 137, 145
Piper P5 115
Poland 25
Ponta del Garda 75
Post Office Headquarters 26, 122
Preston 138
Price, Glyn 14
Prince Rupert, HMCS 80
R100 19
R101 19
Redhill 124
Redlands, Ca 115, 145
Regent's Park 27
Ridley, Bishop 147
Rome 47

Saint, Nate 120
San Francisco 76

Santa Anna 75
Sea King 147
Sealand 108, 109
Searle, Rev. John 117
Segwun, RMS 146
Sesquiplane, P2Y 40, 43
Shepherdson, Rev Harold 115
Shields, Gladys 149
Sikorski, Gen. 65
Silloth 64
Skua 65
Smith, Andrew 149
Smith, Ruth 149
Sola, Stavanger 91
Somerset West 146
Spitfire 73, 137
St Eval 82, 83
St John's Wood 27
St. Martin's-le-Grande 122
Staveley, David 133
Stearman 40
Stott, John 23
Stray, Alan 132
Strong, Trevor 110, 118, 149
Sumburgh 93
Sunderland 66, 70, 89
Surrey 25
Swallow, Bob 13, 14, 151, 153

Teddington, Middlesex 17
Terceira, Azores 72
Thomas, Dr 46
Thomson, W/C RB 69, 71

Thornaby-on-Tees 63, 64
Thornton, Richard 141, 142
Thornton, Sir Edward 142
Thornton, Thomas 140, 141
Tiger Moth 30, 35, 36, 124, 134
Tintagel 151
Toledo 36
Toronto 34, 50
Townend, LAC E 66
Trearddur Bay 124
Truxton, Jim 115
Twain, Mark 86

Valley 108, 134, 135
Vicarage Family 18
Vollendam, SS 32
Voltaire 24
Vos, Norway 145
Wallington, Surrey 18, 20, 23, 27, 122, 124, 126, 128, 143, 145
Walrus 31
Walworth, Jack 143
Warwick 138
Wellington 76, 77, 138
Wesley, John 23
Westbrook 143
Whalley Range 128
Wick 95
Windsor, Duke and Duchess of 60
Windsor, Ont 34
Woodvale 130, 134
Wordsworth 48
York 103